GREEK **SCULPTURE**

"The Golden Years of Greece" taken from The Children's Encyclopedia Vol. 6 Edited by Arthur Mee

THE GOLDEN YEARS OF **GREECE**

The three greatest sculptors of Greece were Polyclitus, Myron and Phidias (or Pheidias). Most of their original statuary has been lost; some fragments remain, and certain copies. The reader might easily ask, seeing that the mass of this ancient work has disappeared, how is it we can affirm that these sculptors share the supreme genius of the world?

The answer to that is Pausanias and a few others, but chiefly Pausanias. He lived in the second century after Christ, was a great traveller, and wrote many books, including a description of Greece. He wrote fully and carefully about the buildings and sculpture, and his history is invaluable. Other men more gifted as writers had composed treatises on Greek art, but much of their work is lost. That of Pausanias was mercifully preserved.

Leave for one moment the thought of the single splendour of Athens in the fifth century B.C.—the Athens which reflected the pure Greek ideal—and think of London today which reflects something of every style of art, good or bad, that has been held by men since Greek art went out in clouds and darkness. Suppose it should happen that a man wrote of London as it appeared to him in 1924, describing its chief buildings and art minutely and faithfully. And suppose one fine day England was overthrown.

THE VICTOR IN THE GAMES WHOSE STATUE WAS SET UP AT OLYMPIA

The victor's wreath—looked upon as the final glory by many a boy of seven yearning for his manhood—was not the athlete's only reward. For certain games a statue of the winner was set up at Olympia. It is interesting to note that only in the event of the winner being successful three times was the statue made to resemble him—to become a portrait. In the ordinary way it was just a type of an athletic youth labelled with the name and honour of the victorious one.

The effect of this "sport" on the sculpture of the day, in Olympia, Argos, and Sicyon particularly, was tremendous. There was always a place in every town where youths congregated to practise for the festival, and there sculptors could watch the beautiful naked bodies to their heart's content. And seeing thus continually the human form, perfectly developed, in glorious play, completely subject to the will, the sculptor could hardly help reflecting this spirit and poetry of movement in his work.

It was inevitable, also, that athletic vigour rather than reposeful beauty, a certain harshness at times, a crudeness, should mark this work of the Doric schools of the Peloponnese in contrast to the Attic school. The whole spirit of Athens was different. The Athenians were a finer, subtler people, more ease-loving, perhaps, certainly given more to mental and imaginative than physical exercises.

PENGUIN
BOOKS
6D

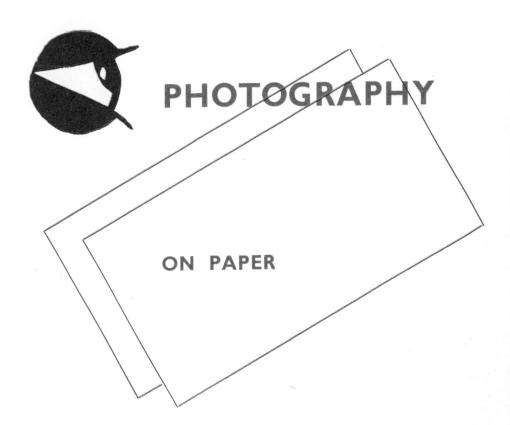

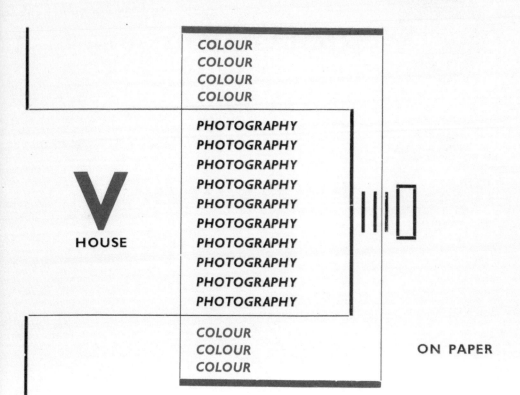

THE NEST OF THE WILD STONES

PAUL NASH

I found my first nest of wild stones on looking closely into a drawing I had made of some bleached objects on the Swanage Downs. It lay just below the level of consciousness, slightly out of focus. But there was no mistaking its lineaments a moment later when I moved the dry thoughts to one side.

I do not think that ideas which come to us from wherever they come should be submitted to analysis, except where there is every reason for, or every reason against supposing that by peeling off the bark we can get at the bite, the bite is better than the bark which is worse than the bite. Or, like stripping a woman to discover the woman underneath.

But if I broke all the shells of all my wild stones I should find that precious yolk which is like precious stones, the black core of the flint.

If stones are eggs they birds are, too. Not even grosbeaks always, or comic birds like toucans, but partridges and landrails much more, and little pretty quails. Larks, even. All birds of the furrow and the down. Sculptors knock birds out of stones. By the time they have done with them they are neither birds nor stones. Except Brancusi's. But the stone birds of the field are always both. They do not insist. Perhaps, when they are lying on the ground they are stones, and when they stand up they are birds, but, thank God, they never look like stone birds.

Sometimes one may find a pair almost side by side. Inseparable complements, in true relation. Yet, lying there in the grass never finding each other until I found them that afternoon on the Sussex Downs, during an attempt to remember whether Edward James lived at East or West Dean. That problem was not then solved, but so soon as my stones came into my hands their equation was solved and they were united for ever. And directly Edward James saw the picture of these two he wished to acquire it. But it is only at this moment I have recalled that these stones came from the downs of West, or was it East Dean?

So life runs on, not cut and dried like some horrible tobacco the Padre smokes, or locked away in an abstract like a fly in amber. But flowing backwards and forwards and throughout; a complex maze of associations which keep the mind guessing, and imagination hovering like that gay summer monster which suggests a nightmare trinity, the elephant-hawk-moth with his inveterate tongue.

Let us kill two birds with one stone. One the egg, one the bird. They are not dead but sleeping; imprisoned in the stone like those truffles in aspic I once bought in the Nice market under Matisse's window. But Matisse keeps all his birds in a great cage, canaries mostly. He seemed to dote upon them, but he never puts them into his pictures, so far as I know. There is a difference between real and surreal birds, of course. But, somewhere in between must come my stepmother's canary which has a forked tail like a Kite or Puttock. I have had the honour of drawing this bird now for perhaps fifteen years. When I last drew him I noticed he had got into the sky. His cage depended from a cirrus cloud. Below, a dark sun suffused the upper air with a roseate film. The cage seemed rather to fly than to be hanging there. With its criss-cross slender bars and perches it looked like a Kite. And then, the other day, I heard the bird had gone blind. Poor bird, he cannot see the sun. It does not matter now, I suppose, that he is in the sky. How is he different now from the imprisoned birds within the stones: they are not dead but sleeping: he is not dead but he is blind. Snarers put out the eyes of birds to make them sing. Bullfinches, goldfinches and larks. I found a stone upon the Downs like a blind lark. A thing choking with song that dared not fly but seemed to strain upwards always. I will make an ivory hand I have fling the stone into the sky where it may sing until it dies and falls down into the furrow.

People say, why do you paint these things? Why are you not content with *things as they are*; applying to them *painting as understood*? All Nature *as it is* seems better so than any imitation of it; than an impression of it, or a post-impression, after all. But we may take the elements of Nature and make what we choose, without reference to existing law and order, or even painting 'as understood'. That seems worth doing, and in result often looks less like a second helping of the English Sunday Dinner than does our heritage of the English Tradition – as understood.

I have taken the elements that go to make my nest of wild stones: earth, air, and hard, cold stone. But of the nest itself, what is there to tell? My first looked like a sheet of squared paper with a torn edge, stretched across a barren field. The next an earthen basin in the hills. But when the authors of *Axis* and I flushed a covey of wild stones on East or West Ilsley Down I found a stone nest bearing the imprint of its only egg. It was a rare find.

But some months later I inherited a small Victorian library more closely stocked with books I do not want to read than I had imagined possible – save here and there a treasure. One such bore the title *Homes Without Hands*. I make a present of it, suitably translated, to Giacometti – with all homage, *Les habitations faites sans mains*. It is a book, illustrated at the height of the engraver's skill, about the nests of animals. The Mole, the Weasel, the Polar Bear, and dreadful Aard Vark and the Mallangong. The Puffin, the Mutton Bird, the Bee Eater, the Gribble and its kin, the Purple Grackle and the Robber Crab. The Piddock and the Shipworm, the Scorpion and the Bird Spider. The Eucera and the Scolia, the Philanthus and the Bembex. The Ant-lion and the terrifying Termites. Nests of a dreadful beauty; under the earth; beneath the sea. Pensile nests, nests which change the face of landscapes. Parasitic nests – the plight of the poor Puss Moth, and the horrid evidence of galls…

A new world was unfolding. Without hands I began to build. I forgot my nest of wild stones.

FORAGING ECONOMICS

DUNCAN MARQUISS

The Jacquard textile loom was developed by its namesake Joseph Marie Jacquard in the early 1800s to accelerate and simplify the production of intricate textile designs. This automated loom appeared at the onset of European industrialisation but it is now considered to be a precursor of today's ubiquitous computer. The Jacquard is programmed to produce woven patterns using a sequence of hole-punched cards; each hole allows a hook to raise the position of the warp thread above or below the weft, determining whether that thread is visible on the surface of the cloth. This method of using discrete units of binary information to control machines is the link between the Jacquard loom and digital technology. The English inventor Charles Babbage is credited with designing the first automated computation machine, which borrowed the Jacquard's punched card system as a means of data entry. Babbage conceived of his proto-computers – the *difference engine* and *the analytical engine* – as labour saving devices that would replace slower human mathematicians.

Babbage was an influential thinker during British industrialisation and became interested in the loss of time and money incurred by industrialists during the training of their workers. His solution was to minimise the need for training by dividing tasks into various degrees of complexity and allocating them accordingly between skilled and unskilled employees. This division of types of labour within the workforce made skill-hierarchies an inherent part of optimising industrial production. Karl Marx identified the division of labour between men and machines as a driving force in the establishment of industrial capitalism, but considered the integration of human labourers into mechanical production lines to be an alienating experience for workers themselves. Babbage's division of labour required individuals to specialise in one specific area of a production process and perform that task ad infinitum. From inside a specialised niche it may be hard to see the larger pattern being woven, or to step far enough back to view the fabric that you're being woven into.

The division of labour is not exclusive to industrial societies, or even to humans for that matter. Social insects such as bees, wasps and ants of the Hymenoptera class all divide labour within their colonies. Typically, this is ordered by morphology; the larger insects go out while smaller individuals stay home to tend larvae and maintain the hive. Yet some multi-generational, or *eusocial*, insect colonies assign types of work to individual insects based upon their age. When insects forage they are exposed to predation and, because of this danger, foraging duties often fall to the elder members of the colony. The economic logic is that it costs the colony less to send older insects on risky expeditions, as these seniors have less potential productivity remaining in them than the younger insects. Through this use-valuation of members, the colony deploys its most expendable individuals to gather food with as little cost to the hive's energy pool as possible. This collective form of optimisation is only possible because all members of the colony share the same genes and, as they are all blood relatives, each individual is willing to risk itself for the survival of the colony. When ants forage, they optimise their collective search effort by signposting the shortest route to a food source using a pheromone scent trail, which is reinforced by the next wave of ants following down the track. This self-organising system reduces the time that ants spend travelling because the longest routes die out as the pheromones fade, while the scent of the optimal path grows stronger through the increasing traffic.

Optimal Foraging Theory (OFT) is an idea in the field of ecology which proposes that a foraging animal will adapt its behaviour to gather as much food as it can in as little time as possible, maximising its net energy intake per unit of searching time. Efficient hunting strategies give individuals a competitive edge and increase their chances of surviving to pass on their genes. As a result, optimal strategies are selected for and become built-in traits. This suggests that an animal's choice of diet is decided by economic factors, based on the availability of a resource and the potential cost involved in finding and consuming it. Some species have a broad range of potential foraging targets, or *search images*. While an omnivore can change its search image, the patterns of movement within foraging have proven to be more consistent.

The term *foraging strategy* suggests a considered plan, but in OFT it refers to implicit patterns that emerge in foraging behaviour. Studies of the flight-paths of foraging animals have observed the recurrence of a frequency distribution pattern known as the Lévy flight, a characteristic long step occurring between random walks. When hunting for scarce resources in large areas, a forager will often revert to a Lévy flight as the most efficient means of locating the next patch of food. To visualise how this pattern forms in the forager's path, we might imagine a bird that feeds on berries flying through the landscape until it happens upon a cluster of berries; it then hops about stepwise, feeding intensively in that patch until the food supply is exhausted, before setting off again on a longer flight to find another cluster. Lévy flights have cropped up in studies of many chaotic natural phenomena, but they have also been identified in models of artificial domains, such as in the fluctuations of stock market indices and in the routes of people browsing the internet. This pattern appears to persist in both our explorations of physical environments and in our searches of abstract spaces.

Peter Pirolli examines the relationship between searching

databases and foraging in his book *Information Foraging Theory*, and claims that our searches for information mirror the hunter-gatherer foraging strategies that we use in the physical world to find food. Pirolli borrows directly from OFT in his model, suggesting that the drive to optimise our searches for useful information causes us to make behavioural adaptations to our media, much as an animal adapts to its environmental niche. In his data-ecology analogy, Pirolli equates information with calories and energy, describing humans as *informavores*.

The World Economic Forum (WEF) published a report in 2011 on personal data that draws comparisons between information and value that are similar to Pirolli's analogies. Yet while he is concerned with how users find useful information, the WEF's report considers the monetary value of personal data that is produced by our traffic with the internet. In this 'attention economy', private companies can use personal data to stimulate demand and generate revenue from their services. The WEF's document describes personal data as a new class of asset 'a raw material on par with capital and labour' that represents 'a post-industrial commercial opportunity'. As information foragers, we search for our individual needs for work or leisure purposes. But our data hunting also generates a sub-capital for other parties, often without us knowing who is harvesting that data. Our movements online leave a breadcrumb trail of personal data behind us that infers our needs, habits and desires.

This information can be collected by analytics companies and sold to marketers who tailor advertising in response to patterns of user behaviour. For instance, the appearances of persistent adverts for hotel rooms in a city we're due to visit after browsing a flight comparison website are an uncanny reminder of this tracking process. Heat maps, software which measures the volume of clicks on different areas of a web page, seem aptly named as they depict the conversion of user's search-energy into data-commodity as a coloured afterglow. These tools help companies to assess the most frequented areas of their site and better position links that lead to *conversions*. Conversion is e-commerce jargon for the tipping point where a site visitor becomes a paying customer – a term that makes shopping online sound almost transcendent. Indeed, the capitalisation on the residues of web browsing has been described by Boris Groys as the 'monetisation of hermeneutics', assembling a ghostly user-profile from the click-streams and effluent data left behind in the searcher's wake.

Alex Pentland, a co-leader of the WEF's personal data initiative, has stated that by cross-referencing personal data from multiple sources, such as location info from mobile phones or credit card transactions, an analyst may be able to deduce a wide variety of outcomes, ranging from whether a person is likely to repay a loan to their chances of developing diabetes. Yet the sheer volume of information now available presents problems for scientists attempting to make predictions. Observing society at a microscopic resolution doesn't produce a smooth curve on a graph or offer rules of thumb. Instead, the fine grain detail reveals the flickering chaos of the real world in all its spiralling complexity. The vertiginous level of information available today threatens to render everything statistically significant. As Pirolli states, we forage in a world awash with information, but such abundance is devouring our attention.

The musical composer and software programmer Laurie Spiegel warns that we cannot increase the volume of information out there exponentially without the meaningfulness of it suffering. Proliferating archives such as YouTube make videos and music so ready-to-hand that they alter how we value that media. It's easy to forget the materials and labour involved in creating these seemingly immaterial cultural transmissions. Particularly when we don't have to look for long to find niche items online, but merely traverse a homogenous interface that dulls our senses to the particularities of each individual entry within the archive. For the pre-Internet collector, the habitual hunting of cultural commodities often constituted a pleasure in itself that extended beyond the obscure objects sought, be it a rare record or out of print book. Beyond any material fetishism involved in collecting, the personal value of an item to a collector may depend on the amount of time and energy they expend in their hunt for it. Internet browsing seems less likely to generate personal narratives of obsessive explorations, but media theorist Lev Manovich has declared that the database has superseded narrative as the dominant form of our time. If he is correct then how we structure archives could be seen as a form of creativity in and of itself. While searching databases relies on filters to reduce the number of results returned, real-world searching uses mental filtering to focus on a specific search-image. Spiegel describes the cognitive system as 'largely a change and threshold detector', explaining that 'if you get a lot of stuff coming at you, you tend to filter out what is relatively constant'. While our ability to shut out the irrelevant signals surrounding us is essential to navigating any environment, our innate filters are now in an evolutionary arms race with the flood of incoming information. Despite this data overload, Spiegel is optimistic about the evolving media ecology, claiming that it will create a paradigm shift into unknown creative models. Pentland also believes that we are in a phase transition out of enlightenment reasoning that was based on averages and aggregates. He states that the challenge for the data analyst today is spotting connections within systems where humans and machines overlap. Paradoxically big data necessitates a more intuitive approach to identifying micro-patterns within that maelstrom. Whilst Babbage's *difference engine* was more accurate at linear computation than its human counterparts, it was not built for parallel processing or to weave analogies.

So what transactions remain between humans and technology that can't be encoded? 'Tacit knowledge' is a term defined by Michael Polanyi, in his 1958 text *Personal Knowledge*, for implicit experiential knowledge that is difficult to articulate. This concept is often used in relation to craft skills and was hijacked by industrial knowledge management literature in the 1990s. Many companies sought to streamline production processes using the tacit understanding of their workforce in order to identify where micro-efficiencies could be made within a production line. Yet 'tacit' means to be silent or wordless, and the transfer of tacit knowledge within the labour process often proved to be a ghost in the machine. Perhaps foraging strategies could be considered a form of silent knowledge. As Polyani puts it, 'we know more than we can tell' about things that we do instinctively. Martin Heidegger's concept of *transparent equipment* – a tool that vanishes from awareness through its habitual use – could also be a fitting description for built-in searching behaviours. Unlike Heidegger's hammer that recedes further from consciousness with each swing, a foraging strategy is an internal tool. As the cyberneticist Gregory Bateson points out, it is not efficient for us to be aware of how we do something while we're doing it, that would require ancillary mental circuitry to monitor ourselves in process. But considering the prevailing condition of data saturation, could conscious foraging strategies help get us to the information that we need faster? Perhaps this forgets that sometimes when we browse online we don't know what we're looking for. In that case, maybe a Situationist style *dérive* through those mediated realms might offer us another means of understanding the economic mechanisms that hold sway within communication networks.

In the chapter on machinery in *Capital*, Marx makes a biological analogy of his own, comparing industry with natural technology, 'the organs of plants and animals, which serve as the instruments of production for sustaining their life'. The WEF's report describes the emerging information economy as resembling a living entity. But how does that system sustain and reproduce itself? Emergent systems organise themselves through mechanisms similar to the ant's pheromone trail for collective foraging, which functions without a blueprint or a single architect to direct it. But, as for us information foragers, it seems that when we go hunting on the internet we aren't just working for ourselves. It would be good to know who else is feeding off our searches.

ADJUSTMENT

ANNA MCLAUCHLAN WITH GERRY KIELTY

AM (Anna McLauchlan): In yoga, adjustment can have a quite a broad meaning. If done with awareness, arguably all actions we undertake can be part of a conscious adjustment process.* However, adjustment also has a specific meaning, where the teacher physically moves the students' bodies using their hands and sometimes other parts of their body. 'What is the overall purpose of adjustment?'

GK (Gerry Kielty): There are lots of reasons to make adjustments. The need for and type of adjustment depends on how experienced the student may be, what type of person they are – where 'type' could mean personality or characteristics such as age, size or gender. As a generalisation, the most obvious purpose would be to position someone in a better place – not to try to 'perfect' their pose, but try to position them in a way that is more respectful to their body, so that they are given a better sense of how the pose should be done. Another purpose would simply be to sensitise a students' awareness to their body, their practice, their breath, their mind, their whole integrated being. There are also some smaller peripherals; an adjustment, which can sometimes just be a touch, is just a very effective way of making that person feel included in a class.

Adjustments are also there to remind the student that you are the teacher. On occasion, students may be led by their ego. For example, you may instruct a modified pose but the student does the full pose. So sometimes I'll make an adjustment to bring them back to that modification, as a reminder that this is not a self-practice, this is a led class.

This links to the role of adjustment in keeping a student safe so they are not at risk of injury. However, adjustment can also facilitate remediation of an injury; it can bring them into a place that aids that healing process. On a more psychological level, adjustments can reassure, so that the students feel comfortable; it can lessen separation between teacher and student.

AM: To the first observation you made about the 'better place'. Can you expand upon that?

GK: A 'better place' is what I perceive as a healthier position. One of the main aims I keep within my own practice (as well as when adjusting people) is to maintain the length of a muscle without compromising the space within a joint. So, for example, you can maximise the stretch of a muscle but, as a result, you can compress the related joint. A 'better place' would be where the integrity of a joint can be maintained, accompanied by the appropriate stretch.

'Better place' would also relate to how I identify the student's body as looking and feeling structurally more aligned. An example would be if a student's back appears to be lengthening as opposed to compressing, or where there's space between shoulders and ears as opposed to shoulders raised to the ears, or obvious things like breath. If the breath is altered, the student can be placed in a position where the breath can become composed and relaxed; if their face grimaces, position them in such a way to lessen the stress they place upon their face.

The question about the purpose of adjustment is quite closed but also open, and it would be possible to discusses this topic is quite different terms. If you go back to the idea of yoga as union – a union of body, mind and spirit – 'better place' could be identified as a place that integrates all those three components. Someone can appear anatomically in a very good place, but psychologically I may sense they are not. So an adjustment, perhaps just a touch, could bring them to a better place psychologically. Again, how do you know if they are being brought to a better place? You just have to go on your judgement and experience.

AM: In terms of judgement and experience, it could be a feeling. But is a feeling different from judgement and experience?

GK: Do you mean 'feeling' in terms of a sense, or an actual physical feeling of when you receive an adjustment?

AM: Sense. But this could be developed through judgement.

GK: I think it is partly a sense. There are also indications that would suggest otherwise: facial expressions, breath, a person's attitude, or other personality-based traits. So yes, I think it is a sense that is partly based on intuition but also on observation.

[Break in recording.]

When you teach someone how to adjust, you teach a standardised form, but that form has to be really pliable because you are dealing with so many different bodies, ages, sizes, genders and emotional beings. And, likewise, when you kiss, that kiss is a pliable communication. That person could be your mother, it could be a lover, or past lovers – it may resonate with all the different ways that you have kissed that person before. As with adjustment, there is an element of intuition and instinct that has to just be there. It's a skill that some people have and some people don't have. People can be taught the mechanics but, personally, my experience is that it's often there or it's not.

Each day, in theory, I could learn another adjustment. To the untrained eye, quite different adjustments can look very similar.

AM: I became very aware of touch after an accident. I have a big scar where I cut my thumb on a table saw and severed a tendon – it had to be reattached. The bone was not broken. There were different physiotherapists at Canniesburn Hospital. One physiotherapist's touch felt very therapeutic. But when another physiotherapist touched me – someone in exactly the same job – I felt a really insensitive pressure placed onto my hand. Her movements created friction and stiffness; she seemed completely oblivious to her touch having this effect.

GK: This is a good example, based on their studies the physiotherapists have probably been told where to press and what to do, yet there is quite a distinction in how you received that touch. Maybe one person simply has that intuitive skill, and the other person does not. Another example was when an ex-principal ballet dancer came to Glasgow to teach a workshop and said to me, 'you have a graceful practice that's either there or not there'. Again, it goes back to touch; for lots of people it's either there or not there. It can be improved, but when you get down to the subtleties… I had a massage from someone who had just started practising, and then had a massage from them some years later. Their technique had dramatically improved. So, obviously, touch can be improved. But, I suppose I'm talking on a much subtler level.

AM: Yes, I wonder about the possibility for change. There's a lot of theory that suggests how you are in the world is a product of different forms of training, and a great deal of that training is unconscious. But I also wonder about that ability to intuit things, and how that then becomes involved in undertaking activities. People can do things in a way that might seem 'quite bad' but appear to get away with it. So sometimes it may not matter how you do things. Perhaps, it's not that it doesn't matter; it's just that it's possible to be something, for example you can still be a physiotherapist, even if your touch seems abrasive.

GK: Someone can be a skilful adjuster, have well-structured classes, be personable, but there may be something that you cannot always articulate that doesn't work for you. It is similar to touch and adjustment, something you cannot always express. How do you communicate something that is so experiential? I could receive an adjustment from someone and another person could do the same adjustment, it might be difficult to say how they differed, but for me, one adjustment might feel more appropriate. It could come down to that skill level, or that person being immersed in the moment, just being very present, perhaps things a student is not so aware of. Or they could have just have their hand there [moves hand to right hip flexor] but if it moves very slightly that microscopic change in placement can make a difference. That's something that you cannot tell somebody.

AM: You have to begin to understand.

GK: It can be intuitive. But yes, you can be really crap and become really good. [Laughing.] I've seen some really uncoordinated kids become really great tennis players through lots of coaching, lots of hard work.

AM: There are aspects to this that are undefinable.

GK: That's the kind of level I'm talking about – those things that are undefinable.

AM: It's interesting when you see potential. I sometimes see it in students, and I also see them wasting that potential. [Laughs.] But I don't really perceive of it as a waste because I don't believe there is one point where potential suddenly manifests itself as a thing, or that it's necessarily better to do particularly well at university. But it's interesting to observe it.

* Key texts such as Iyenga's *Light on Yoga* (1966, Schocken Books; New York) or Swami Muktibodhananda's *Hatha Yoga Pradipika* (Yoga Publications Trust; Munger, Bihar) make no mention of adjustment. Adjustment has been discussed in relation to Ashtanga yoga Mysore practice where the students undertake a sequence of previously learned poses and the teacher guides them via touch (Benjamin Richard Smith, 2007, *Body, Mind and Sprit? Towards an Analysis of the Practice of Yoga*, Body and Society, pp. 25–46).

Dena Yago

I. The Crater
II. Intercession
III. Grinding

I.

Intimacy creates spaces within relations, usurping the place where other relations could occur. It establishes a grey zone where there are no transactions and no one cashes out. Mediation happens in the crater hollowed out by shared intimacies.

Intimacy is traceless; mediation leaves mental checklists, rules of engagements, and other transactional fees. Mediation draws up the contract that stabilises the intimate from its state of constant vulnerability. It de-neutralises the grey space, establishing an exchange – but it is a market where there is nothing to trade, and everyone is left empty-handed.

It is the Judgment of Solomon that leaves the baby as an orphan.

II.

Intercession doesn't give a fuck about the crater. The interceder is a partisan and will act on behalf of one party exclusively. They are guns for hire, working out of their own self-interest. It's generous and noble but not selfless, as it takes a commission. They can be the BFF that's just glad to have their friend back, or the rebound willing to sleep in a still-warm bed. Ultimately, the interceder enters into a client relationship and is motivated by the rewards of success. A more selfless form of intercession can be found in the word's second definition – saying a prayer on behalf of another person. But while the mediator is a neutral body and the interceder takes sides, both remain outside of the sphere of intimacy.

By internalising the role of the mediator and eliminating a third party (possibly in hopes to maintain the closest relationship possible despite the lack of intimacy), it would be necessary to compartmentalise and then to empathise to the point where you could completely lose your sense of self. To this internal mediator, empathy must become an extrusion, a limb that you relinquish control of where the highest hopes for reclamation would only result in prosthesis.

Attachments rooted in all intimacies are formed by agreeing on mutual reliance and accountability (best-case), or dependence and addiction (worst-case). Once you externalise a part of your subjectivity onto an attachment, it cannot be internalised again. It's no longer yours to keep.

There is a term for losing oneself completely to someone in German – *sich jemandem hingeben* – encapsulating a state of complete surrender. *Sich jemandem hingeben* can be translated as literally giving oneself, or abandoning oneself. This connotes an erotic merging, a conjoining of two through one party's abandonment of themselves. There is also *sich hergaben*, the darker lining of giving oneself in disavowal and self-denial.

Sitting on the couch in my own crater, stoned and watching *Blackfish*, I considered the paralimbic region of the brain. In the cetacean brains of dolphins and orcas, this location for emotional processing is far larger than it is in humans. It has been suggested that these animals over identify with the group to the point of having a distributed sense of self. But with these animals, the whole group participates, stranding themselves on beaches en masse. When I have felt close to this, when I have lost myself in a person who hadn't lost themselves in me, I have stranded myself alone, left asking what happens when one occupies a space for two or more?

III.

Grinding will get you nowhere. With a bump, two bodies touch and repel off one another; the grind is directionless. I've been wrestling with how to articulate and document emotional grinding, which could plainly mean intimacy. But the space of intimacy is not a space of negotiation. Creating intimacy doesn't require the application of force, and intimacy leaves no traces (while mediation leaves contracts). Grinding occurs when neither party will give themselves completely to the space between them. It is a selfish attempt to keep something for oneself, and stems from the fear of emptying entirely out into the crater. Unlike intimacy, grinding does not create space. It leaves gristle. When grinding, material creates its own by-product – the granular sediment that's sloughed from both sides.

For one year, I lived in the crater as my own mediator, pouring love into the sphere of intimacy. I would hold the gaping wound trying to keep my love from bleeding dry, while keeping this wound open to other penetrations. Walking through the streets of NYC, my open wound made me porous, the heat of the city softening all edges lowering the barrier to entry. An amputee, I was left with an emotional phantom limb. I wretched in pain with the same force that I'd doubled over in love, walking through the streets seeking sediment as proof that this intimacy existed beyond me. An impression, or what settles to the bottom. Emotional gristle that neither of us could fully own. To fill the third space of intimacy with its sediment, rather than replace it with the rules set by mediation. Regardless of pressure, grinding will not leave an impression, only gristle. Only through the introduction of a tougher intermediary will one side become a positive and the other a negative form. Intimacy is non-penetrative and unclimactic; it is sex where no one comes. Grinding is both the friction that precedes penetration, and the friction that follows intimacy.

It is the soft violence of wilful submission.

Self-sustained vulnerability.

Unnegotiated surrender.

Leaving emotional gristle that is felt between the teeth.

Giuseppe Mistretta

The Impossibility of Ever Knowing a Body Completely

Rauli

You could see it was hot because it was red or there would be areas of red on it. If you held your other hand six inches or so away, you could feel the heat. We did an experiment one day at home to see how far somebody could stand away from me and feel the amount of heat or energy, or whatever it was that was coming off. It was about two feet.

The nature of our hands is that we can feel sensitively. But if you imagine having that amplified more than fifty times, the sensation is so intense it becomes painful. At one stage, if a jumper or a T-shirt brushed against my skin it was a searing hot pain.

Azarole

The rotation of the hand from the wrist he does by eye. There isn't a device to measure that rotation, but he has a device that can measure the angle over the middle knuckles and over this knuckle as well. He's got a tool with a full circle and a straight arm that he lies against my arm, in order to see what the tilt is that I can get between hand, wrist and elbow.

Bullace

The impossibility of ever knowing a body completely because you're always inside it, you can never totally detach yourself, and yet you can see things that appear to be detached from it.

Oleaster

I had to do the exercises in the morning to help combat the stiffness. But if I hadn't done the exercises and I tried to eat breakfast, I couldn't eat with my right hand; I could only eat with my left, and I couldn't get dressed properly because I couldn't hold anything to pull up a pair of trousers or put on my socks.

I had to put the mirror box at a right angle to me, put the non-functioning hand inside, then align the left hand with the right hand I couldn't see in order to fool my brain. What I was seeing in the reflection was my right hand, and by doing that I could touch the fingers without any discomfort. I'm doing it now – I'm looking at my left hand in the mirror and I'm replicating the movement exactly.

The sense of detachment that it gave me because I wasn't seeing skin; I was seeing some other surface. It detached me even more from the limb and I started to find myself thinking about people who have artificial limbs and how they get to know them.

I couldn't extend or lift them or put any force behind them, and he said to me, 'I don't suppose you can rub face cream on with your hand, can you?' I said, 'No, I can't really,' and I wondered why he picked that out as a task that's particularly difficult. So when I was next in the bathroom and

Rauli

When I ran my hand over my partner's body – he's not a particularly hairy man, but he does have hairs on his arms – it just felt really odd. A coarse feeling. Instead of feeling like an act of tenderness, it felt like an assault to myself, which was very strange. It was slightly unpleasant, so I was having to caress him with the good hand in order for it to feel normal.

Azarole

In fact, the medicine I was being prescribed was a very, very low dosage of one of the medications that can be given for depression, so basically what they're trying to do is calm down the whole nervous system. When it's used to treat depression, I think it's five times the amount I would have been taking on a daily basis.

Bullace

They were both standing, her holding his hands while she was gesticulating or expressing something. You watched these two sets of hands and two faces, and you could see him acknowledging whatever it was that was being transmitted by her.

Oleaster

wanted to put cream on my face, I remember trying to rub my hands upwards as you do when you put face cream on, and realised I couldn't push my fingers or keep them straight while I was doing it.

Mirror therapy movements are quite difficult for me, particularly the movement where I'm trying to touch the tips of my fingers with my thumb. When I was in hospital after I'd had the operation, this was one of the first tests they asked me to do. They were interested, could I extend my thumb across my palm, could I bring my fingers down into a fist? I still can't do the latter. The movement of touching the tips of my fingers was very hard at first. It's difficult to imagine now, because I can make my thumb touch my little finger, but at one stage I couldn't. Apparently, the mirror box reconditions part of your brain to remember, which is something I still don't completely understand how the hell it works, because I don't understand physiology, and I certainly don't understand the areas of the brain.

The interesting thing revealed through the programme, however, was that the motivation or the speculation for the way that he conducted all of his research stems from the fact that he himself doesn't recognise faces.

One night he was away, I had come home and taken my day clothes off and put my nightclothes on, and because it was still really cold I put on a warm jumper. I'd devised a way of being able to get out of the jumper by extending my left arm over the top and pulling up. So there I was, I'd managed to get the back of the jumper over my head, I think I still had a cast on my arm at that stage. Anyway, I got the jumper over the back of my head and then got stuck, and I could feel panic rising in me because my right arm was up in the air. The jumper was wrapped over the top of my head, and I was sitting on the edge of the bed. I could feel myself getting hotter and more agitated as I was beginning to see the headlines in the papers saying, 'Woman in her fifties found suffocating in her own jumper.'

He has been trying to make sure that my hand is properly aligned with my wrist, and the wrist to the rest of the arm. He's a kind of engineer.

Through a process of deduction, he assumed she was quite a well-known middle-aged black woman. The kind of photo he was shown made him think she must be someone in the public eye, so he guessed she was Michelle Obama. The second image was Elvis Presley. He presumed it must be somebody famous, but he didn't know who it was. Then he showed him, I think it was Barack Obama, and he said, 'Ah, now I think that's… I don't know who he is,

Certainly, when I was first doing this, my right hand definitely did not look normal. There was something reassuring about seeing what normal might look like again. I wondered how much it was about bridging the gap between what I physically saw and what I wanted to see, eventually, through the process of recovery.

but I think because you're showing them both to me, I think that must be…'. When he saw the picture of the Queen, he didn't recognise her. He said that she looks quite distinguished and quite elderly and, through a process of deduction, she is clearly somebody very famous so it must be the Queen.

In some ways, your hands are one of the things you know best of yourself. Less so your feet, because your feet are very often covered up but, interestingly, I think people do have very distinctive feet as well, so it's interesting that these two bits of your brain are close by one another. It's almost like the external view of your body and the internal one.

The rest of my body was very tired at that time, partly because everything was such an effort, but also because presumably a lot of energy goes into healing. There was my brain and my hand, and the rest of me was rather inconsequential.

Rauli

I guess it really made me think about situations day to day. I'd be gesticulating at people and realising one of the things I was gesticulating with was this ugly object or what, momentarily and unfortunately for me, became this unknown object – something that didn't please me aesthetically.

Azarole

Then, once the right hand started to work, I had to unlearn leading with the left, and learn to lead again with the right, in order to push the right hand as much as possible.

Everything from the weather to how you relate to the landscape. Whether you're a tidy or an untidy

Bullace

In an animal sense, it's about being able to preen oneself. Identified by the physiotherapist consciously or not, it seemed such a fundamental thing to do.

Oleaster

I guess the thing that was most noticeable was the physical distortion of the hand, and therefore its size. Because it was very swollen, I was not able to see the skeletal structure through the skin. I have got quite bony hands, and I'm used to knowing that there's bones inside them. I ended up with a hand that looked like it didn't have any bones at all. It looked more like an inflated rubber glove, or a bigger kind of palm with four or five chipolatas on the end.

person. It's a really interesting process to go through. It actually became quite funny, because it got to the stage where, clearly, I was telling her things that made it quite apparent what kind of 'type' I would fit within, and which range of remedies would therefore be appropriate for me.

You can see it's still not totally right. It's back to its normal size across the width of the palm, and I have a certain amount of dexterity, but I also have a lot of stiffness as a result of the injury and distortion around the small knuckles. Apparently, on my left hand I have what's called an overextension of the fingers, so what I thought was normal actually isn't as normal as I originally thought.

He was interested in looking at how they communicated with one another, and it was all done with touch. They were managing to communicate quite complex concepts and ideas but in a purely tactile way. It was a really extraordinary piece of footage to watch.

I go each week. At one stage, I was going twice a week. We sit either side of a bench that's narrower than this table. We're no more than three feet away from one another, and this man who I don't really know but have come to know, I know through touch. Normally, to sit and hold hands with somebody for forty minutes would be quite an unusual thing to be doing, and it's very intense. Both of us are dealing with it very professionally, but it's a very intimate thing that is exchanged. It's a very generous gift that he is giving, and I'm very grateful for it, but under normal circumstances I wouldn't be spending forty minutes holding hands with him.

Unconsciously, I think I use my hands such a lot that actually it was a bit impossible to try and curtail them, and I also thought, 'I've got to come to terms with this.' By coming to terms with it, so would other people.

I could see why she'd decided on the particular remedy. It was a very weird way of seeing a portrait of yourself. She asked me to describe the symptoms – whether I liked or wanted the hand to be touched, which was an interesting question, because I really wanted the top of the hand to be touched, and still do.

It's almost like my brains had to work hard to remember to pay attention to it. You realise part of the recovery from any trauma is the ability to forget, and that's really important. At the same time, because the healing's not completely finished, I've got to remember to pay attention to it and do the exercises.

What is fundamental to a being's core? What are the bits we can do without, and how does it change us if those bits aren't working properly?

So all of this is going on whilst he's trying to distort my hand in various different ways to make it work. I've seen him now since January, so I've seen him for five months – twice a week. In one sense, I've got to know him quite well and, in another sense, we don't know each other at all.

I suddenly became aware of all the different things I couldn't do because of not being able to actually grasp things. My sense of touch was so heightened it was almost unbearable, which was the effect of the chronic regional pain syndrome, which means that the body's neuro-transmitters – in this case my hand – were over-sensitised.

There was something reassuring about having my hand stroked, but I was saying to her that it felt as if all the energy in the rest of my body had migrated to the hand. It was interesting watching her face as I said it. She understood what that meant, even though if you said that to a doctor they would think. 'Uh, uh.'

VENUS
BLUE HOUR/RED BULB

ELAINE CAMERON-WEIR

Industry came late to the far north, though still heavy, plodding, unstoppable, like a glacier nestled between two rocky mountains, pictured tit-like on the label of the cheap lager favoured by most. The coldest beer with the bluest can and the biggest billboards, enjoyed by the most men in leather gloves, mesh safety vests, and steel toes. Not all of them men really; there was the odd woman, paying for her audacity to work a dangerous and physically demanding job by becoming the object of relentless harassment under the guise of good humour.
Yet enough waves of mostly male workers came crashing down that enterprising prostitutes soon followed, casting into the undertow and setting up camps of their own in the local motels – a lucrative oasis of isolation and high wages. Labourers came, relentless, impatiently waiting their turn to blast old rock with newly piped-in water, the overseers hoping for the dirty brown muck that has lubricated the world for so long, to rain down with the debris. The monumental task of this extraction being spread among so many conscious minds that the guilt became ever more buoyant, each man grateful for the other's presence, as soldiers in a pointless war look to each other to quell any suspicion that they may be murdering innocents. A strange comradery is built out of the mental necessity for these immense networks of manpower; heavy machinery can bear loads but not help with the delicate operation of washing clean a shared, shameful hand in a vast and pointed destruction.

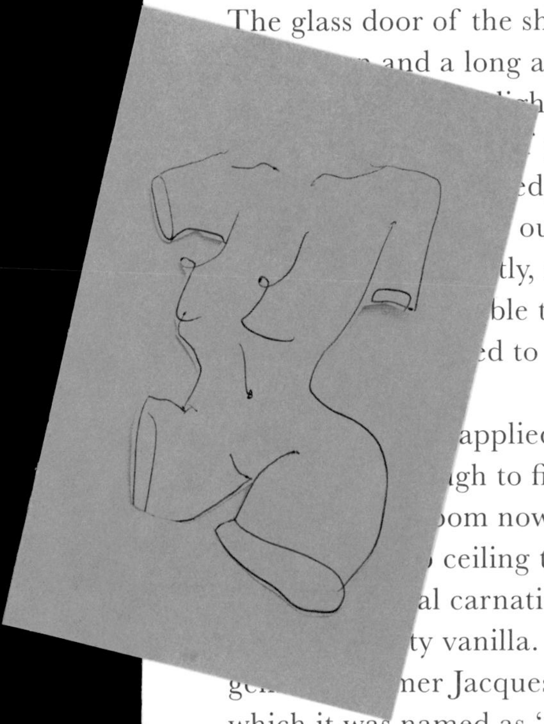

The glass door of the shower, stuck for a moment on its uneven tracks, [illegible] and a long arm culminating in five red points emerges, [illegible] ht bend at the wrist, fingers tented, tentatively [illegible] perfume left somewhere on the adjacent [illegible] ed, the atomiser is given a hard squeeze sending [illegible] out and over the threshold, past the edge of the [illegible] tly, settling over her neck, arched back in automatic [illegible] ble to the habit of the procedure. Her breasts, [illegible] ed to nothing save youth and genetics.

[illegible] applied, she has mild anosmia; the scent of L'Heure [illegible] gh to fill a small-town high school gymnasium, let [illegible] om now saturated top to bottom, from worn pale-pink [illegible] ceiling tile, with its slightly melancholic, nearly-too- [illegible] al carnation and anise accord, followed by the delectable [illegible] ty vanilla. Launched over one hundred years prior by [illegible] ner Jacques Guerlain, who described the time of day for which it was named as 'the suspended hour', L'Heure Bleue had gone through several recent unfortunate reformulations in an attempt to appeal to the 'modern woman', a figure invoked by advertising, but only defined as a set of vague insecurities. She prefers the vintage stock still bearing the intelligence of its creator, undiluted by focus groups, and undulled by the desire to appeal to a homogenous femininity that did not exist. Often, she found herself scouring perfume forums online, searching second-hand shops and flea markets for half-used flacons of the golden liquid. She enjoys lining them up in ascending order, according to year, and selecting which to use as a pet method of supplicating immaterial transport to the corresponding year of vintage.

The intermittent ritual of wearing perfume, the application and evaporation somehow marking time and breaking it into reasonable fragments, much like the satisfying punctuation of chronology achieved by smoking cigarettes. She had smoked Lucky Strikes for twelve years, first aping the supposed taste of entrancing cinema goddess Marlene Dietrich while impressionably young and working at a dilapidated theatre in the Mid-West that exclusively screened old movies. It was never busy and she often spent shifts chain-smoking on the balcony to catch up on all the glamour she had missed, re-watching *Blonde Venus, The Devil is a Woman* and *Desire* night after night until eventually the theatre went out of business and she moved on, taking her new addiction with her as a souvenir.

The combined olfactory effect of L'Heure Bleue and Lucky Strike cigarettes was nearly pitch perfect; the shimmering qualities of the perfume brought more to life in contrast with the dark acridity of the tobacco smoke, the mingled silage winding a bright trail after her, like a long-exposure photograph of lights moving through darkness. Languorous, luxuriating alone in a seduction without audience, she lifts a cigarette to her lips, still naked, warm rivulets of water sliding down her limbs and pooling on the tiles at her feet. She is deliberate, slow, the lighter popping to full staccato flame just as 'The Midnite Sun – Vacancies' sign clicks on for the night, the neon tubing buzzing and blinking in the azure twilight.

The phone rings from the bedroom, startling, though muffled through the closed door, now opening with a heady puff of steam. Smoke and perfume curl out after her gesturally, as though she had gotten away, already one hand on the receiver, the other adjusting the cigarette, preparing to answer. The first call of the night is coming in unusually early, but she's ready and she takes a long drag so as to answer coolly on an exhale, voice slightly lowered. She plans to pause briefly then say 'hello', with no upward intonation at the end, no query or question, as though she's been expecting the call.

'...hello.'

'The intellect distorts thought by framing information
into concepts
This is not an adequate measure of what can or cannot be
And when the electric light of the ego burns,
The candlelight of intuition cannot be seen in the room
in my messy bedroom
Saturn Returns at roughly 29 years old

```
MERCURIAL vapourised mercury in neon tubing to create
brighter light
argon gas, myrtle leaves\\\backslash backslash backslash
mighty mighty aphro die tea.'
```

On the other end of the line she hears a low buzzing sound, followed by a few short clicks, then silence summed up neatly by dead air and a dial tone. Rolling her eyes, she puts the receiver back on the cradle, completing the exhale as though movement in her ocular cavities drives gears elsewhere. She stretches out supine on the bed, beside the phone, wet hair soaking the pillow, her eyes closed now, lids lowering over the pupils which, in turn, rove over the inside of the lid. Spots of light remain fixed there, owing to the eyes that inadvertently rolled past the bare light bulb hanging from the ceiling.

It was a vulgar energy-saving bulb, likely the only thing in the room that had been changed in several decades – another regrettable upgrade on a par with the reformulation of L'Heure Bleue. She detests the quality of this light. Its serpentine coils produce a clinical blue white far too bright and possesses the odd characteristic of making blood appear orange, as though what exists under it was inhuman. At this time of night, she usually replaces it with a soft red bulb that mimicks the effect of candlelight, blurring the edges of things, making the cheap room appear a little richer under its glow, much like the effect of the L'Heure Bleue, in which everything is submerged and marinated. The pinkish wash of light also had the desirable result of making bare flesh appear indiscriminately flawless.

She brings her right arm over her eyes, the inside of her elbow shading her face and relieving the garishness of the light momentarily. With this same movement she brings the cigarette, now extinguished, to the ashtray perched on a squat night table whose sole purpose has thus far been to hold, in its first drawer, an extremely neglected Bible, and now, periodically, a red light bulb. Rolling to her side, she opens the drawer, retrieves the bulb temporarily relieving the scandalised New Testament, and sets it carefully next to the ashtray as she glances at the clock, 7.48 p.m. Bringing herself to stand barefoot on threadbare carpet, she strides slightly on tip-toe back into the still-steaming bathroom to retrieve her half-packet of Lucky Strikes.

Lighting a new cigarette, she catches her reflection looking back at her from above the shell-shaped sink, her naked torso appearing to rise from it. The chrome faucet just covers her pubic hair with the hot and cold taps sitting like sentries on either side. She looks squarely at herself, allowing the flint lighter to stay flipped open and lit, flickering, illuminating her breasts and face from below, creating an unfamiliar visage, half visible, blinking back at her through the dissipating steam. Leaning slightly forward, inhaling, she wipes condensation from the mirror flatly with her palm, twisting her entire arm from the shoulder socket, creating a half moon that comes to frame her face.

The gesture provokes a dim memory, an inescapably transportive wave of déjà vu begins to loom, and she braces somewhat for impact by slightly lidding her eyes. Dust from the past blowing over her: walking aimlessly under a leaden sky, the sun just below the horizon, but the stars not yet appeared. Foot pain, stemming from the excessive use of high heels, slows her gait. Getting in a parked car and smoking, always smoking, behind the wheel, and surrounded by the familiar dysphoric glamour of L'Heure Bleue faded to its brackish sweet powder and singed crayon odour. An odd light in the sky above, visible through the sunroof, she can't be sure of the source. She looks up in her reverie, tipping her eyes back in their soft sockets, and sees herself far away, from above: an indistinct outline, and a sound increasing in tempo, gradually, like it is wound up until only a single tone persists. The duration of a thousand nights, time-travelling in a parked car. A natural means to a man-made purpose. A vessel to fill. Held in her mind's eye in this twilight transit, she takes a drag, momentarily fixing down the transparent layers that occasionally overlap to create corporeal opacity.

Her reflection comes into focus now, the steam gone from the room. She sees herself clearly again: eyes half-lidded, mouth half-open, exhaling. The smoke curls from her nostrils slowly, like some great monster moving at half-speed.

The phone rings abruptly a second time, the sound popping into the room as though the air is viscous enough to bubble, heavy with the omnipresence of perfume and trance. She blinks hard and jerks her head back a little, the same micro-movement performed countless times in startling moments of presentness, then fleeing the bathroom she bounds to the phone. She abandons her customary flat tone this time, instead answering eagerly, unable to conceal her concentrated desire to return to the present and to practicality.

'Hello?'

'the line fixes itself, repaired perimeter, new outline, bright light
a totality and a singular point
we've all felt something sometime
birth of Venus coming true
it's down the drain
it's up in flames
real clear like a bell ringing or a pendulum swinging
heavy boot at the end of the leg, hypnotic
it's real Italian leather man, Italy the boot jutting peninsula, then
an eye opening in slow mo, heavy-lidded bedroom eyes for some moments,
stretching open farther and farther still
until the slow horror of the wide eye reaches its zenith
and what's there is a dark iris so dark it's black against the white
like a negative image of the moon on film
looming stark and full.'

Again, no answer. The line goes dead but she does not hang up. She begins to scrutinise the room from where she stands, as if she cannot locate a hidden reason in her surroundings that might explain the repeated emptiness on the other end of the line. Her eyes travel over the rumpled bed with its wet pillow, worn wooden chair to the left, over which her panty-hose and underwear were tossed after being peeled off together, and now the crotch faces out like an eye looking back at her. Directly left of the chair, on the floor, a pair of black leather boots, a gift of Italian-made luxury from a long-suffering still-infatuated admirer with good taste and the income to fulfil it. Bunny-eared television atop a cheap laminate-covered cube, a luggage stand, uselessly stationed near the door, smudged and filthy around the knob; it reminds her of when she worked as a chambermaid at a resort in the Rocky Mountains six years ago. Fired for using the telephone in guests rooms while on the job, racking up phone bills, mostly calling her younger sister out east via long-distance, and occasionally indulging in the odd television psychic. But now she hangs up briskly and hurriedly, lighting another cigarette. The audible precision of the snaps and clicks of her actions act as punctuation to finalise and dismiss the terrible silence.

The phone rings a third time and she snatches the receiver off the cradle, nearly shouting, by now annoyance causing her voice to rise almost imperceptibly, slightly sticking in her throat.

'Hello!'

'duration of a thousand nights, time-travelling in
a parked car
natural means to a man-made purpose, a vessel to fill
what is freedom
inhaling she wipes condensation from the mirror flatly
with her palm
twisting her entire arm from the shoulder socket
creating a half moon that came to frame her face
eyes half-lidded, mouth half-open, exhaling
the smoke curling out from her nostrils slowly,
like some great monster moving at half-speed
whose practised somnolence betrays
the immanence of violent expenditure.'

Once again, she hears nothing, the caller seemingly refusing or unable to speak. It unnerves her, this unexpected feeling of disarmament, provoked by the absence of a voice on the other end. More disconcerting than the unknown motive behind repeated silences. She speaks slowly through clenched teeth, baring them a little by curling her lips up at the side and fully articulating the sharpness of the quick consonants, and drawing the two 'S' sounds out, giving them a menacing snakelike quality: 'Sstop calling thiss number.' She slams the receiver down viciously, taking a hard drag of her cigarette and running her hand across her forehead, rubbing her right temple, blinking rapidly.

She steps up to stand on the bed, its worn springs softly squealing under her feet. Reaching for the coiled bulb, she gingerly twists it out of the socket, severing the electrical connection and sending the room into near darkness. The faint light of the unextinguished wind-proof flint lighter, its hinged lid left open, could be seen emanating from the bathroom. Picking up the red bulb she twists it into place, the red light flickering for a moment, echoing the movement of the flame. She looks up closely at the light, squinting and tightening it in the fixture to prevent it from wavering again, cigarette hanging from her lips.

Descending from the bed, she returns to the bathroom to snuff out the lighter. The phone rings. She looks up sharply in the mirror, her thumb snapping the lighter closed. She cannot see her face, eclipsed by an orb of hot residual light, imprinted temporarily onto the rods and cones of her eyes, the red blind spot persists in the centre of her vision. For the first time there was an intoxicating potential, an unbelievable strange beauty now terrifying in its clarity. Otherworldly and unquestionable, influential as the moon pulling tides of adoration over and over, lapping at her feet which stand in puddles on the tiles.

WHEN THE EARTH ENTERS YOU – MOVEMENT AESTHETICS

FRANCIS SANZARO

I. JOYFUL CONSENT

For over twenty years, I've been building a very particular type of body. I've been training it to deploy force in contradictory ways, slow down at certain intervals, and move in manners that ordinary life will never require. I've been training and developing my muscle to exert with reckless contraction very near – and sometimes past – its breaking point, but also to settle seconds later, regroup itself, and continue in a state of relaxed aggression.

As a rock climber and, more specifically, a boulderer (a gymnastic form of climbing), what I've been training my body to do is, in a very literal sense, receive ecology, embody weather, and perform an act whose script I've never read. This performance takes place inside the realm of movement – a third term between body and stone. To be able to inhabit movement – to react, generate and interpret the affects within this space – is the life work of any athlete. Having spent decades climbing it, and years sculpting it, stone reaches out to me intelligently, pleading for a duet, regardless if I am exhausted or depressed. I always consent, joyfully.

II. RESPONSIVE BODIES

Contemporary web design uses the term 'responsive' to describe a website's ability to excel in any environment, such as a phone, tablet or a computer. When loaded onto a new platform, a responsive site changes its font, colour pallets morph, and structure adapts to its new environment. The proliferation of platforms or digital environments has made this a necessity.

Historically, it is no coincidence that so many contemporary sports, including surfing, skateboarding, and parkour, are practices of responsivity. It is no coincidence that in an era of the death of touch – an era where the ancient skills of the body that allow a landscape to enter it are becoming extinct – generations have been attempting to revive this skill. As a sport of touch, landscape, skin and mutuality, bouldering is thriving in our era for obvious reasons. The bouldering body does not actively reach out to the world towards a passive block of stone. Rather, the body goes to stone as an instrument seeks a musician.

Likewise, new strides in technology speak of *smart materials* – materials whose properties can be altered as a result of changes in their surroundings. Walk fast over one material, it feels like concrete; walk slow over the same material, thereby producing less force, you sink as if in clay. Smart materials respond intelligently to tasks and processes set before them by changing their qualities. And while we are amazed by them, we forget the smartest material of all is something we carry around on a daily basis: muscle.

Muscle alters its qualities and behaviour when different forces act upon it. When your muscles work on a flat surface for long enough, you get the qualities of dance. With a four-inch surface, you get the routines of the balance beam. Ice produces certain movements not possible on pavement, and so on. Of course, there are a lot of things to do on a beam other than gymnastics. More to the point – muscle is not just the athlete's smart material, it is the body's smart material. The only difference is that the athlete has learned to exploit muscle's qualities with greater dexterity, working on it and being worked by it, a matter of coaxing, perhaps even persuading it to release its affect with greater intelligence, onto, and within, the body.

Smart material produces forces internally, all the while navigating external forces. The bouldering body does this so well that, at certain times (and as we near the limit of our ability), we become indistinguishable from these forces. Muscle *produces*, as there is no time in the day nor any movement I do when I am not reminded that my body is a climber's body. It is co-present with my life, a glaze of potentiality that my body has been dipped in.

While smart materials alter their qualities for specifically designed purposes, to what purpose does the body change its qualities? Most would say that a dancer's body changes its qualities to appear more beautiful, but what is beautiful to a spectator is often an entirely different affair for the dancer. A performance can be a dreadfully painful affair, and yet the audience sees effortless grace.

Muscle *is* responsivity – we shall begin with that.

III. DUMB MUSCLE

Given all the fashionable theorisation of body, materiality, surface, touch, molar/molecularity, flesh, plasticity, carnality, and so on, it is a strange thing to see muscle sitting there, in a corner by itself, with no one to talk to. More than likely, we refuse to speak to it because of the cliché that muscle is 'dumb'. But it is the muscular system that allows us to bat our eyes in love (or disappointment), or move our hands across another's back after they have experienced tragedy – movements requiring such sophistication that they can only be orchestrated by an autonomous, responsive 'intelligence'.

As Deleuze noted, one must begin from clichés. The clichés spring up immediately in our mind: muscle is a slave to consciousness – simply a support. It is meat, a brute, unthinking substance. It is a display of hyper-masculinity, a substance of power and forced will, of will to power.

It surrounds our body for pragmatic and survival purposes, or, in modern times, for aesthetic purposes (the body building spectacle; greased pecs, defined quads, glorious beach muscle). Simply by calling attention to it, one makes a statement. Muscle rivets us to the body, excessively.

Class distinctions aside, it is true that muscle is 'ignorant' because in the face of resistance, it only wants to get stronger. This is what muscle does when it meets resistance – it builds more tissue, capillary beds for blood and connections for recruitment. Yet, this does not make muscle dumb, but smart.

Give a beginner a tennis racket and tell them to hit the ball as fast as they can. Their movement will be inefficient, sloppy. The strength that they do have is mostly wasted. In time, strength becomes a means, not an end, in this activity. But we must ask ourselves: *to what end* does it get stronger? A dancer's body gets stronger, but to what end? A dancer does not want to *simply* get stronger, that much we know. And to say that it becomes more beautiful is to think like a spectator (this spectating position limits possible thoughts on such a topic). What does strength mean in the case of bouldering, which is analogous to dance on so many levels? It would be a cop-out to just say the body learns to do more difficult things.

A question more important than *what* it wants to learn (since there is no one thing) is *how* it learns and the changes it undergoes to receive that knowledge.

IV. THE GOLDEN THREAD

A body never ceases to move, and neither does stone. A boulder is a wave that takes a long time to crash, and boulderers 'ride' that wave for a bit, in full acknowledgement of its fragility. Perhaps unique to our sport, a legendary performance can be erased with the strike of a hammer, or frost heaving, since the performance changes with even the most minute of alterations to the stone. On the other hand, a rockfall or mudslide can create new performances, as did the recent boulder that wrecked a centuries-old Italian farmhouse only to land gently in a field in Ronchi di Termeno.

When we boulder, our fingertips settle into a hold formed by thousands of years of rain, weather, rock type, sun, wind; our toes cringe on small edges in existence for hundreds of thousands of years. Our consciousness need not register observations, but our body is ingesting them. Just as the surfer's body experiences the unique force of riding a wave which has no beginning, but which has the beginning embedded within it, so too the boulderer's body knows the history of a particular stone by how it feels on our skin, how much friction it has, how its holds are shaped, and so on. Every boulder is a recording device. They age like trees.

Our bodies feel, hug, scrape and curse their way up these stubborn behemoths. We pant, our legs sputter, and since we face the stone alone, our backs are turned to others who watch us struggling like death. In our struggle, we can only fault the stone to the extent we fault ourselves, since, as we grapple inches from its surface, it appears silently complicit to let us fail; the boulder's strength is our weakness. You learn stone has temperaments, preferences, attitudes, styles, behaviours and colours. While the boulderer must invest large amounts of time to inhabit a boulder's surface, often there is a vacuum of temporality on either side of bouldering movement; we sit patiently for days, sometimes weeks, underneath a slice of stone going over potential movements. The entrance into movement begins with stasis, with a ritualistic breath, with an acknowledgment that the past begins when movement commences. Yet, when we are finished, movement does not cease – since our bodies continue to move – but rather that this genre of movement closes. The closure is a second stasis where the compressed movement catches up to us. What defines this movement is not the clock but the elements that have become part of the movement assemblage.

Bouldering is also a dialectical imprinting, a mutual downloading of a complex organic structure composed of affect, energy, body-type etc. On the one hand, this performance, created with materials of a varied history and ecology, is a tapestry of effort, elements and love. It is personal and eccentric, whose 'centre' lives in the person who did it first. These original elements find themselves interpreted in us. On the other hand, it is impersonal and concentric, with a shared centre that lives and breathes only to the extent that it is continually downloaded from the boulder and uploaded into a communal memory. These performances only live when they are enacted.

The performance goes forth into the world of bouldering as a shadow, activated only when another's effort shines light on those holds, on that surface in geology. In a literal sense, the unique performance required to climb its surface is millions of years in the making. Bouldering movement upon such a structure is therefore marked by an elastic stretch of temporality – a golden thread, as it were – in which the performance at once spans a geo-atmospheric history and a scripted performance to be shared in an open-ended future.

V. REMEMBERING GEOLOGY

How is geology remembered then? For starters, it just is. The body remembers the moves geology has produced as sand remembers a rain – it is a process of co-production. The body does this willingly, without labour; i.e. *responsivity*. As with electric, shuddering sex, the body carries the performance around all day, presenting itself in the form of a 'running' image-affect beneath one's primary layer of consciousness, only to intercede upon the day with delightful phantasm, to say nothing of the survival reminders of fantasy.

This is about how the body responds to repeated acts of touch over decades. Just as the over-sexualised body becomes infused with sensuality, wherein every act is an occasion to exercise this tendency, so too one cannot escape a body built for specific purposes. After a certain time, athletic bodies take part in a de-fetishisation; the entire body becomes built for a task and, equally, the entirety of the body becomes open to the forces that the cultivated body produces. For bouldering, the body parts that contain the most nerve endings are the lips and the fingertips, and so, by a mixing of metaphors, our hands literally taste the world.

Just as an increased heartbeat is the manifestation of a hill, so too the flat surface is deeply embedded in the dancer's body, not only physiologically, but aesthetically. The quads, glutes, hamstrings – all these are marks of the floor, of what it takes to jump (with grace), lift (with ease), or spin (with balance). For a climber, we are marked by a boulder: calloused hands from friction, swollen knuckles from too much grabbing, over-developed forearms from hanging, ballooned rear deltoids from climbing steep walls.

A distinguishing feature is that our apparatus is *not of our creation*. Yes, we decided to climb on it when we could have chosen to do other things, but we made a decision to climb something in which the manner of climbing is not decided by us. It is the boulder that determines how you climb it, never vice versa. The boulder has arrived to us in history, a product in process.

It is said with regularity that dance articulates (as can football) social categories. The femininity of ballet reflects social norms of gender difference, even down to the postures. In 'The Ballerina's Phallic Pointe', dancer Susan Foster writes, 'she extends while he supports. She resides in front and he remains in back. She looks forward as he looks at her.' In other words, dance movement has within it implications not necessarily produced from the floor, since a man could move in a more feminine manner, but does not.

In bouldering, there are no social categories because our genre of movement is not socialised – getting to the top is all that matters. Yes, *getting to the top* is a social convention, of sorts. In gymnastics, for instance, gendered convention has given us the beam, but in bouldering our apparatus cares little for gender. But, then, won't gendered bodies simply use that apparatus differently? It doesn't appear so, at least not in an aesthetic sense. Our sport requires that we try hard in any way possible, regardless.

VI. A REDEMPTION, OF SORTS

In *The Botany of Desire*, Michael Pollan makes an argument, which goes something like this: all the sweetness in an apple was produced by the apple, in order that the apple can continue its genes. We would pick it, so *it* (not us) could stay alive. We think we are picking apples, when it turns out apples are picking us. They change themselves to become more attractive to us, to satisfy our basic yearnings.

To think that ecosystems, of which boulders are a part, do not also seek to reclaim their health would be myopic. Of course, boulders are inorganic entities. They cannot alter their composition, as an apple could. But that doesn't mean they don't have a life. While we will never know what boulders 'want', what we do know is that the bouldering is an act of protecting spaces – spaces of touch, joy, struggle and fitness. Organisations now exist to buy boulders, and protect them and the performances they offer from development.

Like any artistic process, a boulder provides a seductive material populated with pre-determined behaviours, and boulderers work with that material until a performance is created, a performance that is equal parts history, individuality, sunlight, passion and vulnerability. The bouldering performance is then a mutually composed script. And while it would seem natural to say that a body goes to stone as a musician goes to an instrument, the truth is that, in the act, it is impossible to determine who is playing who. It is equally hard to discern who is protecting who. Landscapes use us.

Will Holder

The Recessive Subject

(Second draft*)

* *This is the second of three published drafts, rewriting pp. 42–45 of R. Bruce Elder's* The Films of Stan Brakhage in the American Tradition of Ezra Pound, Gertrude Stein and Charles Olson *(Wilfried Laurier University Press, 1998). A previous draft appears in Luca Frei's* Thursday followed Wednesday and Tuesday followed Monday and there was Sunday and there was Saturday and there was Friday *(Spector Books, 2014). The final draft, for children, will be published in* F.R.DAVID, *'Dit–Dat', Summer 2014.*

The sentence can be described as a complete unit of thought. 'Amy listens', subject-verb, its most elementary construction. The subject is 'Amy', the verb: 'listens'. Introducing an object to a sentence constructs subject-verb-object, the standard or *canonical* word order:

'Amy is listening to the song.'

'Amy', is the subject, 'listening to' is the verb, and the object is 'the song'. The subject names what the sentence is about, the verb tells what the subject does *or* is, and the object receives the action of the verb. In certain cases a 'linking verb' will describe the subject, 'Amy is enthusiastic', or rename it as the object of the sentence: 'Amy is a copyist.'

Amy pays no heed to her body as 'a medium of experience' while she walks down a busy street. Yet unconsciously she steers it around lamp posts, bicycles, people and other objects. We call her subject-body *recessive*. It needs to be in order for things to make themselves aware to her. That is: Amy's subject must recede, or withdraw while it mediates the world. If 'Amy observes her subject-body' doing this, it comes forward (to become both subject *and* object of her attentions) and as such, is no longer recessive. As it does, she'll just assume that – like herself – other subjects are recessive, with her as their object, and move out of her way.

The recessive subject is essential to bodily skill. We've all experienced Amy practising a new dance-step, until she stops thinking about how to get from one move to the next. Similarly, if she became aware of every movement of her right wrist, hand, fingers, producing every stroke as 'Amy sings what she memorised', or 'Amy copies down what she sung', the song will no longer be the sole object of her attentions, and none of us will sing.

SORT OF LIKE A HUG: NOTES ON COLLECTIVITY, CONVIVIALITY, AND CARE

PARK MCARTHUR

For Tina

On 13 August 2011, which was a Thursday – no, the calendar says it was a Saturday – I bought a notebook.[1] Inside it I wrote:

> *a space to process care collective stuff – be open with myself – in combination with what I'm reading about dependency and care with or vs. justice. 'Collective' feels like using a language adopted – a language I am trying to learn – as I learn how to operate in a collective in general. A collection of people. A collective.*

The week prior to 13 August was my first experience participating in a care collective: a group of nine people working to help me shower, change my clothes, and get into bed each night. Nine individuals – seven people for each weeknight, two people to swap in when needed – built and sustained this collective.

Throughout the fall of 2011 and the winter of 2012, I wrote in this journal almost daily, so regular was my need to record these initial experiences receiving care in this way. Outlined here is what was established and what continues to be created. This account seeks to

[1] 13 August is Catherine Harrison Walker's birthday. She turned 28 in 2012. She is one of my closest friends. We met twelve years ago in college. She moved from New York to Nashville, Tennessee, yesterday, 5 April 2014. Her birthday is 13 August 1984 and mine is 14 September 1984. We moved to New York together in the late summer of 2010. My parents paid the rent of our apartment. I went to an art programme called the Whitney Independent Study Program and Catherine worked at Whole Foods. Catherine provided all of my care from August 2010 – July 2011, except when we weren't together (as when one of us was out of town). Our relationship, and the way that it layered living with care with rent, was one of the things that encouraged my thinking about receiving care from a group of people. This kind of arrangement (parental financial support for housing in order to receive care from my roommate) is still how one of my current roommates, Amy, is asked and agrees to participate in my care.

describe the form of care collective (cc), as well as the relations that formed it and were formed by it.

To be clear, this account of care and connectivity is not about an intra-disability community or about relationships formed between people with disabilities. It is about a group of people – only one of whom identifies as disabled – caring for me, a person living in New York City with a diagnosis characterised as degenerative and neuromuscular. Unevenly descriptive, this incomplete narrative seeks to frame questions I have concerning care's obligations and desires. In an effort to think about interpersonal care on a social scale, I map my specific experiences of physical dependency onto queer theorist Jasbir Puar's outline of 'convivial' relations. Convivial relations consider categories such as race, gender, and sexuality as events – as encounters – rather than as entities or attributes of the subject.'[2] Without forgoing what identity categories and processes of identification offer, this essay focuses on types of relations coded as 'dependent', and the experiences, feelings, and knowledge such encounters with dependency engender.

CARE AND ACCESS

The first time I received care from a rotating group of people who were neither my family nor people I paid was as an attendee of the 2010 US Social Forum in Detroit, Michigan. Five, occasionally six, friends shared a hotel room for the week-long event. Our group did not formalise a schedule of how and when to provide care, but kept in close touch with one another, trading off anticipated jobs: helping me in and out of bed and the bathroom, meeting up for meals. The labour of care was by no means portioned equally between each person sharing the hotel room; the people I was closest to emotionally shared their time with me the most regularly.

Across the city of Detroit, in the Wayne State University dorm rooms, organisers of the conference's Disability Justice Track

[2] Jasbir Puar, 'Prognosis Time: Towards a Geopolitics of Affect, Debility, and Capacity', *Women and Performance: a journal of feminist theory*, vol. 19, issue 2, pp. 161–172

created a care-shift collective called Creating Collective Access (CCA) http://creatingcollectiveaccess.wordpress.com/. CCA, whose organisers invited individuals to pool their resources, skills, and abilities, was envisioned as:

> *a community-built-and-led collective access network of crips and our comrades, wanting to help create access in ways that also build community, care, crip solidarity, solidarity with non-disabled comrades and is led by crips!*

Care girded the structure of CCA, and it determined the pace of living together in Detroit. Each person's daily care needs were folded into each day's rhythm and activities. CCA attempted to keep care self-determined and non-exploitative. It sought to make care group-negotiated. This shift in the discursive and organisational parameters of justice indicates an understanding of reproductive labour's inherent relationship to any praxis of solidarity.[3]

Organisers of the US Social Forum – like many groups using a one-to-one customer service approach to accessibility – provided hand-outs and hotlines for questions concerning structural access: which buildings and forms of public transportation were available to people getting around on wheels; where to locate roomy elevators and gender-neutral bathrooms. Access needs were addressed through the circulation of information to people perceived or self-described as benefitting from this information. But CCA – and most disabled people, for that matter – plan for the realities that enliven and trouble the common denominator of structural access, foregrounding the caring labour needed to complete structural accessibility's promise. The promise of access and egress can often only be fulfilled with another person. Accessibility is social. How does one use public transportation if maps are illegible and directions difficult to remember? Who will be there to

[3] Though collective care, as part of social justice movements for disabled people is somewhat recent in both its articulations and its practices, there are many examples of groups and organisations that place reproductive labour at the centre of organising forms and processes. For decades, and mainly through the necessity of collective childcare, feminists across nations and political campaigns have highlighted the ways in which care is integral to social justice.

make transfers to the toilet within the ADA-compliant bathroom safe? If the Forum's convention centre houses thousands of people – along with their noise, their motion, their activity – who will be a calming counterpart? These questions of touch and weight, relationality and recognition interrogate the psycho-somatic, phenomenological, and haptic fields and feedback loops of public and private life. They are questions sublimated or ignored in conceptions of public life, unaccounted for within rights-based discourses, and largely unrecognised within formulations of just societies. They are questions that do not end at the end of the workday. They are not answered by the hiring of a sign language interpreter for a half-hour of programming.

In America, part-answers to these questions have been historically situated and bound to private family life and/or the State's administering jurisdiction – two spheres of social activity maintained as repositories for the excess leftovers of capitalist accumulation. The people whose lived realities call these questions into being – and, of course, the questions themselves – remain, for the most part, politically obscure and socially atomised. Such questions involve intention and consent, dependency, safety, exploitation and abuse, translation and effect. Such questions are concerns of people who receive-give-need-want care. They animate the relational, intra-personal, asymmetrical, non-reciprocal, non-recuperable parts of life.

The work of people who receive-give-need-want care outlines an ontology of care. Care, as a term that does not intend to ignore its own politics of language, describes a spectrum of dependency and labour different than childcare, different than elder care, and different than the heteropatriarchal configurations of an unwaged labourer reproducing a waged labourer for tomorrow's workday. In this case, I mean the labour required of individuals caring for adults who can not reproduce themselves vis-à-vis the systems and working infrastructure that grant an individual the appearance of independence. Adults who do not reproduce themselves vis-à-vis such infrastructure are often characterised as disabled. To acknowledge the tenuous, collapsible relationship between debility and capacity – within both disability and non-disability alike – proposes an ontology of care not yet socialised and theorised, much in the way that philosopher Laura Hengehold writes, 'our bodies should always be better than the societies we currently have.'[4] Without ignoring the importance of the societies we currently have or could have, this quote speaks of a future that flips the assigned metaphors of disabled fire alarms and paralysed systems of an insane marketplace for a world in which every disabled, paralysed body and insane mind is already better than the conditions we take to be their linguistic approximation. Setting aside a body politic to talk about bodies and minds that always exceed a politics means caring for ontological being – caring for flesh – along a spectrum denser and more complex than what passes for our fanciest thought-projects.

Care is a plastic term. Care Studies's acceleration as an academic trend does not mean someone necessarily wants to identify themselves as 'needing care' or as a 'care worker.' Campaigns for domestic worker justice, for example, show how the term can be used to exploit workers by placing an emphasis on work by a 'family member' rather than the work of an employee for her employer. In campaigns for disability rights, the term care is understood to be infantilising and antithetical to struggles for self-determination. Additionally, the caring labour of a gendered, non-protected constituency of citizen and non-citizen workers is made as recuperable as possible to home health and healthcare industries.

But in CCA, as in many kinds of kinship networks, the question of two or more bodies in correspondence with one another – care-receiver and care-giver – push access further afield from its traditionally understood legislative base of equality, anti-discrimination policy, and structural access, towards generative grounds of communal commitment, collective affinities, identities, labours, and desires. Articulated and theorised as 'access' in addition to 'care', CCA lays bare the relationship between these two realities. When care *is* access, access is made to be a communal effort and constitutive goal of personal and group care. As a condition of justice, care-as-access prioritises something else other than the limitations of rights-based accommodation and anti-discrimination policy: it seeks to understand and nurture the social realities of reproductive labour.

[4] Laura Hengehold, *The Body Problematic: Political Imagination in Kant and Foucault*, Pennsylvania State University Press, 2007, p. 300

I did not participate in CCA, but heard about it, read about it, witnessed it, admired it, and compared it to my own hotel room version of group-provided care. I think about it now as it exists in various iterations around the United States, including this experiment with my own care in New York City. Like CCA, my care is a group-based effort, both in how it came to be and what it is.

Seeking regular care from places other than biological family, a monogamous partner, government agency, or private business means casting a net wider than the people I live with, wider than professional home health agencies. In New York City, Consumer Directed Services, a weekly email and website maintained by Edward Litcher, circulates the needs of individuals seeking to hire care providers www.consumerdirectedservices.com. This online entity's main audience is disabled people as well as professional care providers, both Medicaid-certified and not. Not knowing of Consumer Directed Services in 2011, I sent a series of emails, Facebook messages, and listserv announcements describing my care needs to friends, acquaintances, and strangers. To each respondent willing to share two hours helping me, I offered money or a skill I could provide in return. Seven friends replied saying they would participate, giving their time without remuneration. Four strangers agreed to initial meetings. Post-interview, two of the four individuals began working with me for fifteen dollars an hour.

Finding care-givers within social communities to which I am loosely linked makes apparent whom I spend time with, for what reasons, and with what openness we allow work to enter our relationships. The majority of people who care for me are artists, academics, educators, or non-profit workers, many of whom are queer, with a day-to-day capacity to be with me past nine o'clock in the evening. They are white, in their 20s and 30s. Our ages are proximate; they are not caring for someone far older or younger than they are. Care collective members share mutual friends and professional ties, apartments, and connections to each other through people and organisations unrelated to me. Crucial to the success of cc's hybrid form is the foundational care my roommates provide. My roommate's ability and commitment to getting me out of bed in the morning, every day, eliminates the need for someone to be at my apartment at 8 a.m. My other roommate – my younger sister – who is also disabled, coordinates her care needs in collaboration with mine.[5] Both roommates' patience and flexibility make my weekly care schedule possible – a schedule supplemented and interrupted by close friends who come for dinner and stay to help me afterwards, by my bandmate after band practice, by someone I have sex with, by visitors from out of town.

Care collective is a collective endeavour insofar as it requires seven people working the week's seven days, but we do not spend time all together; some participants have yet to meet each other. We haven't yet made decisions collectively. Care collective is not a collective in the ways that a communal house or organisational structure commits itself to yanking at edges of hierarchies in an effort to topple gendered, classed, and race-based divisions of labour. It is, however, populated by people already committed to reconfiguring social relations in the ways they choose to live and work. A number of participants care for people with disabilities, people old and young in addition to the work they do in cc. For others, our weeknight together isolates their physical care work to a few hours of time.

Across this spectrum of caring labour vibrates a charged interest in what possibilities exist or are created in the ways we relate to one another. The relational events we make cross and re-cross divides of nakedness and coverage, emotional closeness and reticence, attention and bored inattention – manifesting as actions that look like embracing, making dinner, drinking alcohol, cutting hair, falling asleep, reading poems and essays, watching YouTube videos, massaging limbs, recounting stories. These activities ornament the basic goals of showering, changing into pyjamas, and getting into bed. My own interest in these acts of relating scale disparate spatial and temporal registers – from the shapes our bodies make during a lift-and-transfer, to the alternative commitments we decline in order to meet at the same time and place.

'Collective' is likely a misnomer, a pseudonym for something else

[5] My sister and I no longer live together, but she and her husband (whom she now lives with) provide support when gaps in my care schedule arise.

finding its form, its routine and sway within sequential, differently-shaped chains of day-to-day, one-on-one pairings. Care collective situates my care requirements centrally, around which additional needs, desires, and force fields orbit and pull.[6] Processes of unravelling and restabilising occur as we make ourselves vulnerable to one another while working to deliver our bodies safely from platform to platform, surface to surface. The strain of someone's body lifting mine; my body's strain in keeping myself upright; learning how they, as the bearer of their bodies, and I, as the bearer of mine, work our mutual instability together. I observe, and am given, this open materiality as an instructor of my own care. I compartmentalise my discomfort and desires in order to describe how I want my shirt to be lifted over my head. I experience my care partner's translation of this request into motion and pull. I say I will be home at 9.25 p.m. and I am late. Someone waits for me. Or I wait for her. Rarely comfortable mergers such as these ask us what we want from each other, despite the fact we are most practised at conceiving of the care we provide one another in terms of needs.

EVENTS AND EXCHANGES

Care goes alongside life itself – an always ecology, an often commodity. The effects of care's commodification strain and make violent the relationships between people giving and receiving care. These violences are heightened as caring labour is de-centred from contemporary life through rigid demarcations of how much support one can need and still be considered 'adult', 'productive', 'worthwhile' on one side, and what kind of work one does in order to be considered 'adult', 'productive', 'worthwhile' on the other. De-centring care from its social ecology also creates an avoidance of end-of-life care that can only be repurchased as an exploitative commodity. When one is not able to maintain and renew

[6] As we gather, couple, and link ourselves to one another through reproductive labour, particular movements and durations effect the ways we relate to one another. By this I mean the ways that we feel with one another, and the ways we feel one another, which, for me, within cc, is different with each person and, therefore, different each night of the week.

her world by herself, the task becomes how to involve other people's labours in her world-making. As an adult in need of substantial, sustainable, and increasingly committed care, I am recognisable as a life worth caring for, a life worth preserving through resources and labour taken and distributed to me. I asked my adult communities to care for me. They said: 'OK'. But behind this 'OK', this 'yes', echoes a chorus of 'nos' – the 'nos' I hear and have heard personally, and the 'nos' more widely directed at most people needing long-term care.

Caring labour and dependency demand we think 'couple' and 'collective' simultaneously. Or, put another way, prying into the ways care is beholden to obligation and desire generates multiple trajectories. Within cc, I experience the process of incorporating care into existing friendships as well as the process of incorporating loving friendship into arrangements first based in care. Encountering each other not through the intimacies of fighting or sex, team sports or rivalry, care-as-event obeys and follows through transferences of weight and fluid and affect, creating, over time, an aesthetics in addition to an ethics. Born of dependency, these events' ethics are a holding and being held, an attention and an attending to that are sustained through tomorrow and tomorrow's tomorrow. Constitutive of each event is the reality that care must be repeated and replicated. And safely. What haunts any open materiality of bodies as places to meet (Puar's description of 'the event'), are these meetings' quantities and qualities – the fact that events are both numbered and textured. Events navigate sensitivities, variables, and factors in bodies' meetings – meetings are not ahistorical or atemporal but are often set up through ideological, state-approved calculation. The real and potential destruction of bodies across time and space is any event's contingent prediction.

The social realities conditioning care today renders it a matter of class access. Social death occurs when care is withheld and exploitation is made routine. Though violence inhabits care, the ethics beholden to an ontology of care is not a matter of 'good' or 'bad'. The ethics described earlier concern the event itself, not whether care is good or bad or if a caring person is better than a non-caring person. Rather than 'good care' and 'bad care' there is 'care' and 'not care'. Or 'care' and 'without care'[7]. For example, to describe care collective to strangers and acquaintances is to routinely hear 'wow, you must have incredible friends' in a response that affirms my friends' goodness. My friends' perceived goodness, their decision to help me without pay, sits inside an ethical expansiveness generated by an ontology of care that finds reproductive labour everywhere. It is true my friends are not only incredible, they are the best people alive, but it is care's everywhere-ness, care's everyminute-ness that is ecological, not moral. An ontology of care makes 'good care' a redundancy.

I wager care collective is, most likely, not a replicable mandate for new forms of sociality. Too many particularities exceptionalise its existence. More importantly, the kinds of relationships described here already exist and will persist after cc dissolves. But cc is a playing out of what need-based, care-based relationships between disabled and non-disabled adults might be – a playing out of what adult peers do and *can* do together is what notates care collective's conviviality.[8]

CONVIVALITY

Conviviality, as a potential ground for group formation, expands collectivity's colour-coded categorising, its distribution of skills and identifications assumed to be even, similar, self-contained, and consensus-based. Again thinking through Puar's essay 'Prognosis Time: Towards a Geopolitics of Affect, Debility, and Capacity', care based in dependency invites or, more specifically, requires inequivalence and

[7] On pp. 50–51 of her book *The Life of Poetry*, Muriel Rukeyser writes, 'a work of art is one through which the consciousness of the artist is able to give its emotions to anyone who is prepared to receive them. There is no such thing as bad art. [...] It seems to me that to call an achieved work 'good art' and an unachieved work 'bad art' is like, calling one colour 'good red' and another 'bad red' when the second one is green.'

[8] I want to be clear that I am not proposing non-wage care work done by friends as a more socially or economically progressive alternative to waged domestic work; my friends' capacities to care, are, in fact, dependent on the time and energy available to them in addition to their jobs. It is this tension and slide between community-based care and non-wage care work that I want to think through. I do not want to reproduce the precise logics of gendered, classed, and raced exploitation in the name of 'alternative care structures', nor do I want to think about unpaid care relationships as 'outside of' economies of care presently in need of further regulation and wage increase.

asymmetry to produce uneven relations, events, and also the place from which I write: the squeeze. There is the squeeze, and there is the mandate. There is the loop of two arms anchored at my lower back, legs on either side or in between mine and a charged space, a space somatic but not exclusively sexualised, smooshed breasts and chests, arms that change with the days but come back within a week. And then there is what is compelling about something useful and something ordinary. To share something that I can't make sense of on the occasion that someone else can assign it meaning and utility beyond what it already serves me. I write from the squeeze, but I also write from my anticipation of the squeeze, a readying. I write from its release, too.

Care collective will change its current state; it may disperse entirely. Dispersal and dissolution is the promise of convivial relationality. As Puar writes, conviviality is open to its own 'self-annihilation and less interested in a mandate to reproduce its terms of creation or sustenance, recognising that political critique must be open to the possibility that it might disrupt and alter the conditions of its own emergence such that it is no longer needed'. This is true for the care group as a whole, for participants' relationships with one another, and for my relationship with each person. Convivial care expands and refines ways of being together, ways that don't seek care solely in relationships among partners, children, biological family members, or relationships mediated by government agencies or not-for-profit entities. Conviviality is also a project that feels like a thesis – not a conclusion, or even a proposition worked out, but an old definition of the same forcefully sonic word: a thesis as hands or feet keeping time. Not only counting, but counting down. 4, 3, 2, 1, hit it.

POSTSCRIPT

A version of this essay was presented at the conference 'Cripples, Idiots, Lepers, and Freaks: Extraordinary Bodies / Extraordinary Minds' on Friday, 23 March 2012, at the Graduate Center of the City University of New York, as part of 'Cripping Community, a panel moderated by Akemi Nishida (Critical Social Psychology PhD candidate at CUNY, and cc participant).

Since then, I've reshaped large parts of the essay three times. First, to re-write the paper's ending after my friend, an artist and cc participant Tina Zavitsanos, said that to invoke survival as I did in the original essay's last sentence, seemed both unnecessarily tragic and vague. Then, in seeking contemporary psychoanalytic theory's help in understanding cc, I added professional writers' voices to the essay, namely Leo Bersani and Adam Phillips, from their book *Intimacies*. And finally, for this iteration, the other writers' voices were removed, and a postscript was added in order to focus on what a singly-authored narrative about group-created care means when writing something to which I am simultaneously witness, participant, and subject.

Though such processes of editing and re-editing are hole-making, there is also, everywhere, the presence of patch-makers and their patches. I rewrote and rewrite this text as I learn things: the patch-makers being my teachers. The teachers being people I know and don't know, their lessons being a casual comment, a serious conversation, a decision to continue or not continue participating in care collective, the social movements for care and labour justice at large, an academic paper read at a conference, other accounts of friends' experiences with care shared socially. I couldn't not alter this essay after experiencing changes to the form of cc while thinking through what those changes mean. In many ways, this essay is all a postscript.

I edit this text because it dissatisfies me. The language and concepts I use to describe care and its relationships dissatisfy me. Partial descriptions and inconclusive commentary show how much I want to show how much cc matters, past and present. Both how, and how much, it has made me. What else it makes.

'What else it makes' is a placeholder for my desire to talk about what we're doing together, now – what we are together – when it feels that so much attention is given to the potential, the possible, the future, the receding horizon of action and significance. Care makes us now. So difficult is it to be attentive and sensitive enough towards our events, places, experiences, and occurrences as we deal with them and as they deal with us, that descriptions and assessments of these events may only produce bogus theories. I want the bogus theory. I want it instead of the repetition of 'might' and 'possibility'. Contingency is not only a quality and texture of futurity. An already-thereness is a reality and a constraint to be taken as given. I edit and re-edit this text to be wrong, to be more precise in the ways I am wrong in order to provide a place for additional re-edits and accounts other than mine to land.

Since 2011, cc has changed and gained participants; people have joined for both long and short spans of time. Participants move away from New York and also return. New York City has allowed cc to shift and shrink, grow and morph in ways difficult to imagine occurring without the city's communities of artists and its critical mass of disabled people living close to one another, its public transportation, its accelerated relationship to knowledge and information. Void of any one of these components, care collective might not be able to reproduce and respond to itself.

I participated, for example, in a friends' short-term care collective in the fall of 2012, not as the provider or receiver of care, but as someone who connected other people to my friend. This temporary collective was organised in response to the power outages caused by Hurricane Sandy. To make plans around my friend's and his partner's needs after the hurricane meant joining a collective of dozens of people living across the United States. In communication mostly via text but also online, the networks to which I am connected supplemented the collective's main group of care providers. I called on groups of artists and acquaintances to purchase, find, and deliver supplies to lower Manhattan and to drive my friend's care providers (some of whom lived in New Jersey and Queens) to and from his downtown apartment. Many people did a part of each activity in order to accomplish necessary goals: providing a car-ride one way, or picking up and delivering one supply item. This short-term care collective was initiated by two participants who also sustain my collective. Parts of this care collective's activities are recorded here: *http://littlefreeradical.com/2012/11/04/unconventional-aid-helping-nick-dupree-part-ii/*

Mary Simpson

Soft Footage

The measurement for any image
begins at the film plane.

Focus is determined through distance: measure of ground, light and air; measure of manner and agility; measure of the optical path from light to lens.

-

Mark the distance to the film plane: of aerial image (viewing chamber) to eye, and of aerial image to lens.

Determine which rays of light will be in focus. Invert them. The margin becomes the centre – not the viewfinder intersecting a frame, but the oscillation beyond it.

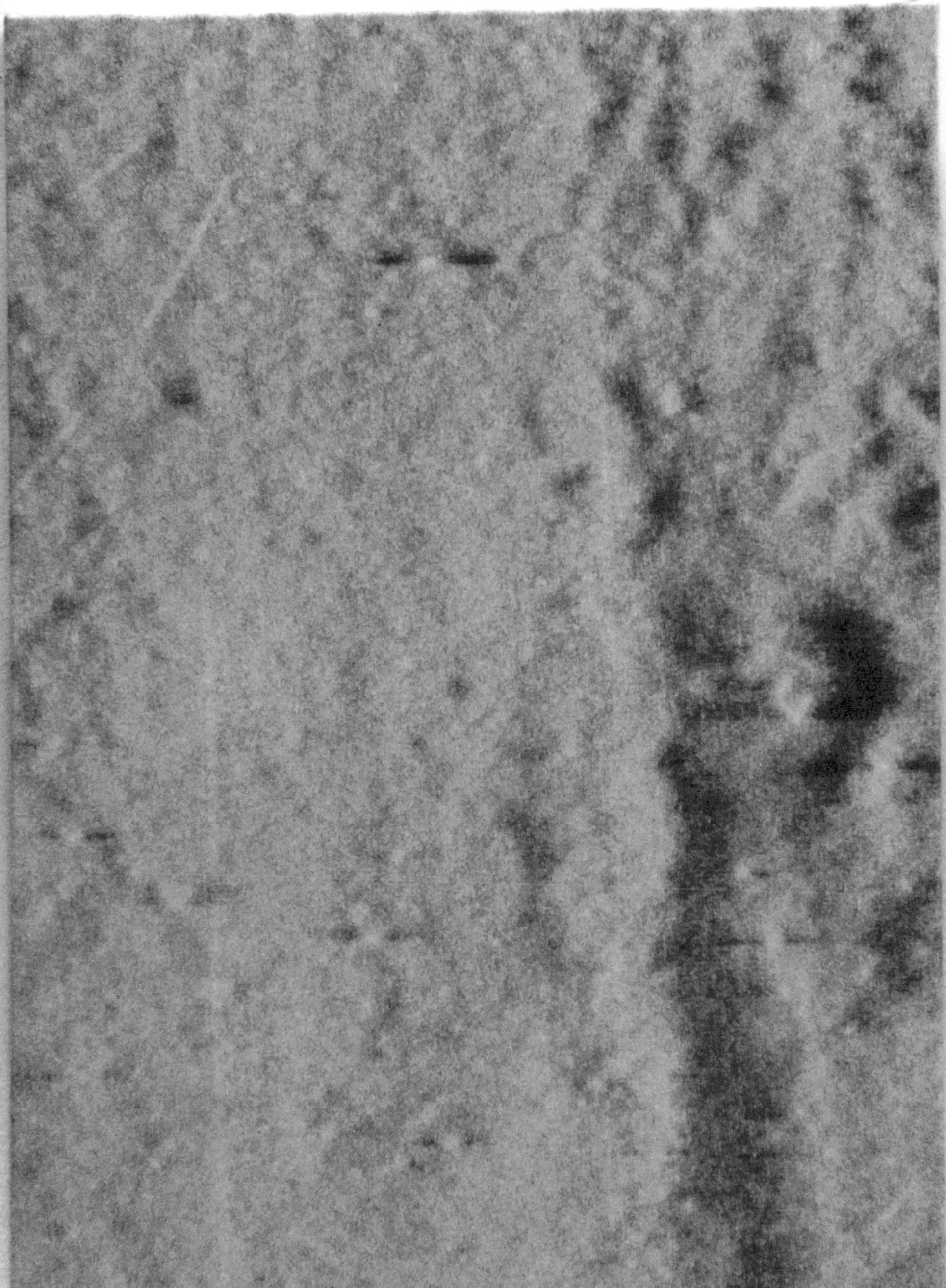

Mark the line suspended from
image to film plane. Measure
the part of the body in focus
– not an image of the body,
but a body for the image.
Transfer this measurement
to the lens.

-

Follow light through its
optical path until it enters
the lens. Mark the lens,
not the eye.

Any marks made to judge
distances will become the
mental map of this moment.

The eye will never meet the
accuracy of the lens. Muscles
of the eye will work
independently from mechanics,
pulling the image into focus
while the body remains soft
on the film plane.

-

The eye will see a focused
image where none exists. The
eye can hardly be trusted.

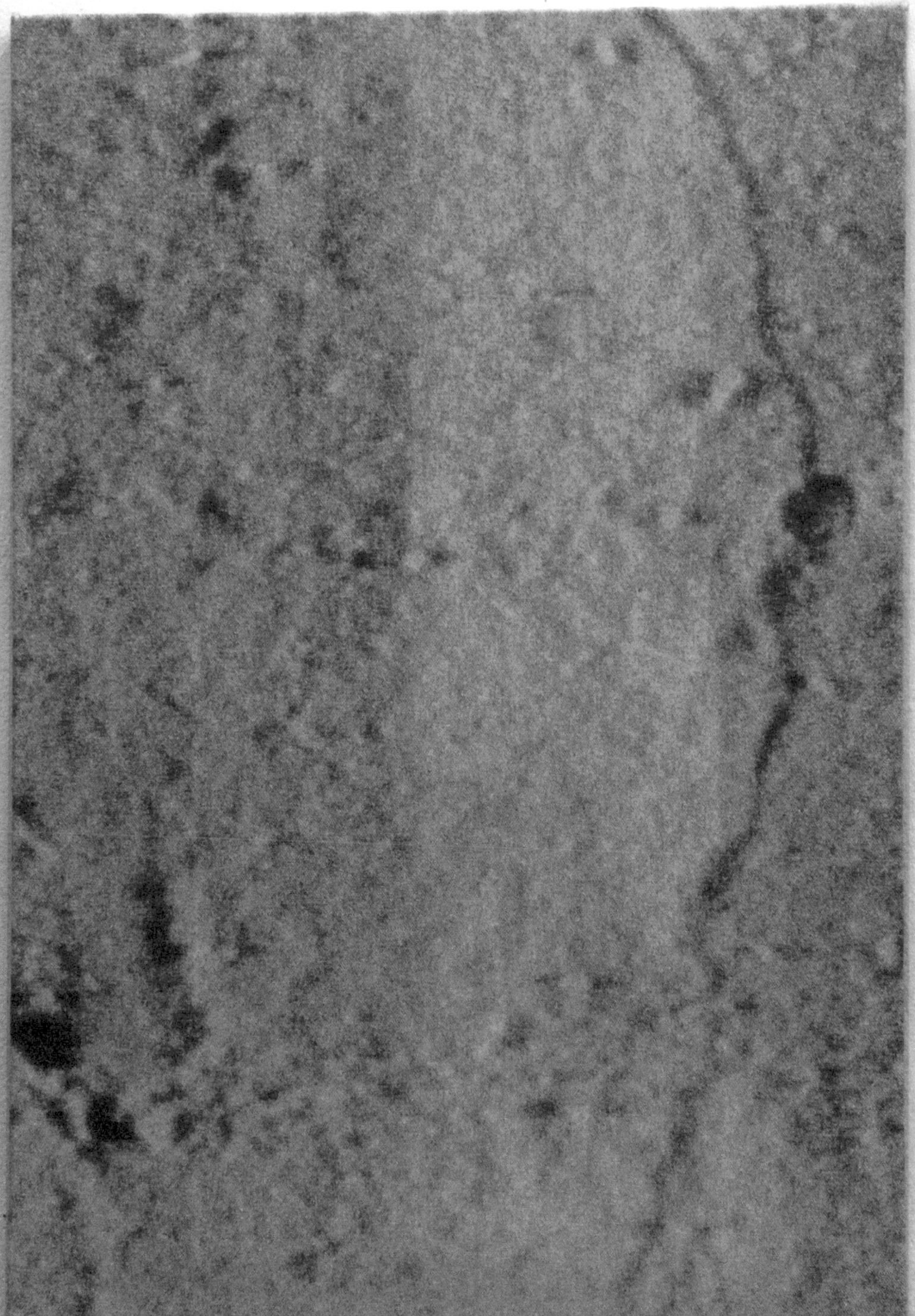

Soft footage. This means that to dilate the temporal moment, a returning arc (lookback) will cause the moment of the look that ends gesture. Turning to salt or stone. Halting movement. The image is mortified, the image is stuck in the throat.

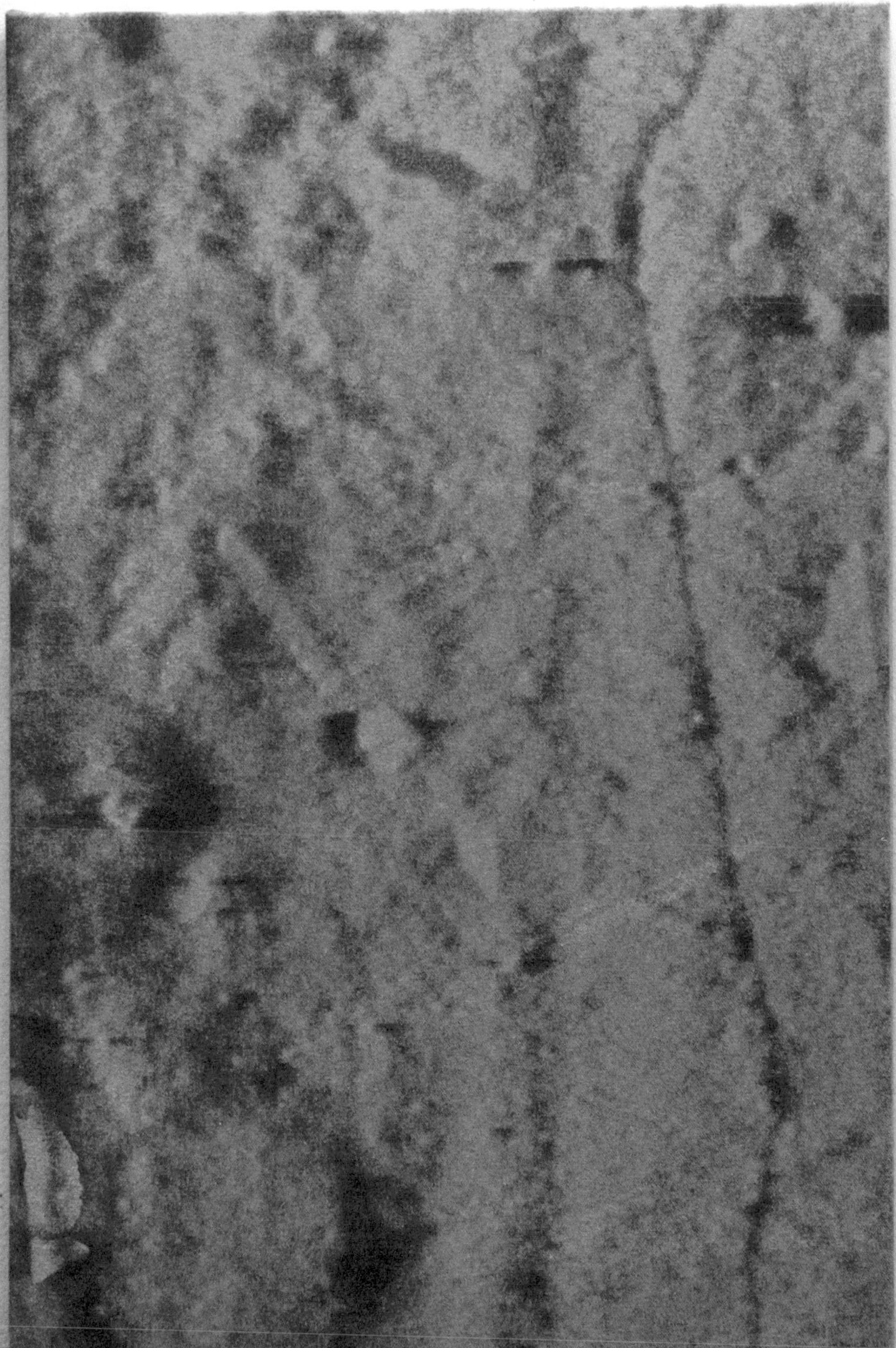

Persistence of vision
requires the retina to see
links between images that
don't exist, to arrange a
line of movement that isn't
there, *l'émouvoir*. The margin
becomes the centre.

To keep an image out of
focus, mark the suspension
between inhale and exhale,
the intervening pause between
contracting heartbeats,
between sensation and
thought, between one thought
and the next, during the
inability to think. Dead
time. *If I presume to know
you, I've killed you in
my presence.*

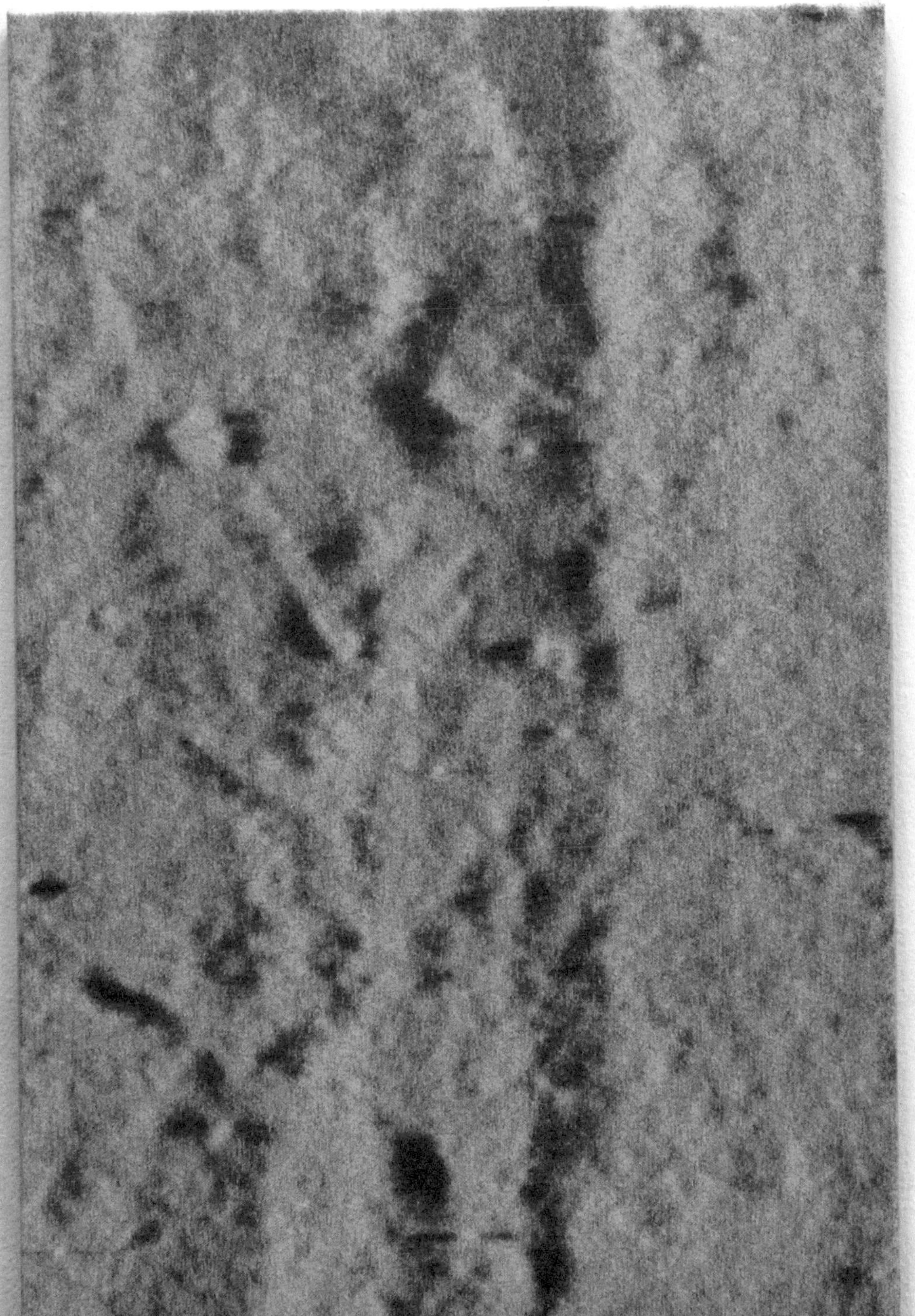

Allison Gibbs

Spirits of Ecstasy

In 1929, the film director F.W. Murnau relocated to the Polynesian island of Tahiti to make what was to be his final film, *Tabu: A Story of the South Seas* (1931).

Tabu is divided into two chapters – *Paradise*, chapter 1; and *Paradise Lost*, chapter 2 – and registers as an unambiguous conflation of German Expressionist and ethnographic filmmaking, of the dramatic and the naturalistic. The film's protagonists Matahi and Reri (played by Matahi and Anne Chevalier, respectively) were both local to Tahiti, and both continued to work in the film industry following the release of *Tabu* (Chevalier was already embedded within the entertainment circuit of Polynesia prior to *Tabu*).

A black-and-white silent film, shot entirely on location, *Tabu* was made at the threshold of the colour 'talkies' boom. Murnau originally conceived of it in collaboration with documentary filmmaker Robert J. Flaherty, and to be financed by Colorart following Murnau's split with Fox Film Corporation (due to what he considered to be a creatively oppressive, albeit financially successful, partnership with Fox). However, following a series of disagreements regarding plot and the complete loss of support from Colorart, Murnau directed and funded the film alone. Flaherty continued to work on the film's processing and editing, along with cinematographer Floyd Crosby. Apart from Crosby, Flaherty and Murnau (in addition to Bill Bambridge, who played the role of the police officer in *Tabu*), the film's technical crew consisted entirely of local men, woman and children. Following production, Flaherty sold his share in *Tabu* to Murnau, and the film's distribution rights were purchased by Paramount. Seven days before the premiere of *Tabu* in New York, on 11 March 1931, Murnau was killed in a car accident.

His death had been prophesied by a clairvoyant Murnau visited in Santa Barbara, as well as by a Tahitian seer. Before his body was returned to Berlin, Greta Garbo commissioned the making of Murnau's death mask.

The superb skill of the Maori wood-carvers was also used on their great war canoes. The prow shown here is over four feet high.

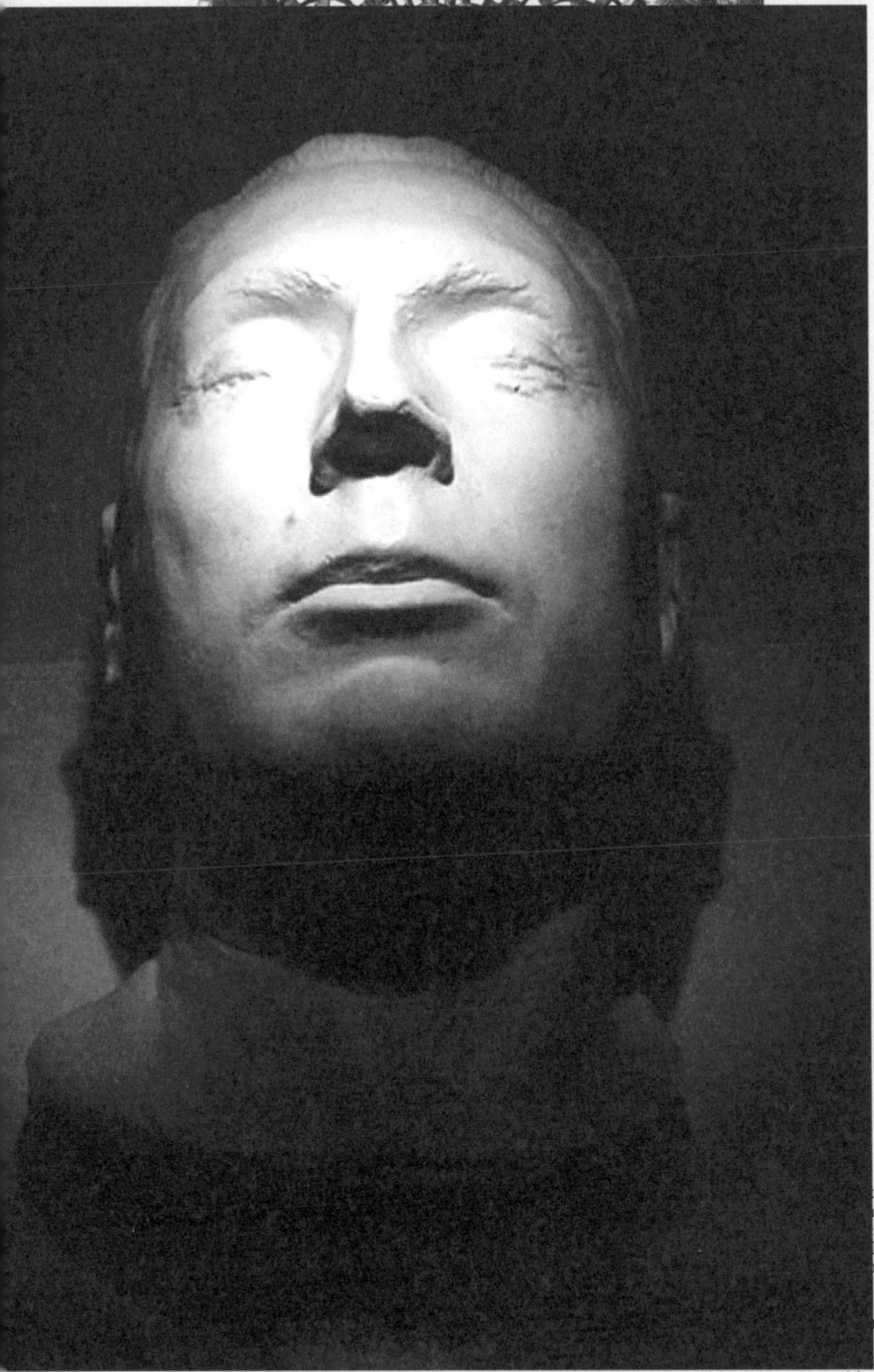

: Rarotongan ironwood image god, collected by the London sionary Society and labelled Rongo and his three sons'. There ns some doubt about this as Rongo is not known to have three sons, although the nearby ngaian Islanders say that Rongo three sons who were ancestors he Ngariki tribe. Some authorities believe this to be another figure of the god Tangaroa in the act of creation, an idea supported by the presence of the smaller figures. British Museum.

with fine sennit braiding, to represent him. They were not impressed by Tane-the-chirper. The affronted priest carried his god off to the island of Aitutaki.

human sacrifices were made. The idea of stability which his name also implied was reflected in his role as assistant to Ta'aroa, the creator, in the myths of the Society

I am approaching an island. From the sea. And the shape of the island is singular, imposing. The high land of the interior unites in single mass, rearing into a form that resembles a double-peaked mountain. The elevation is perhaps 3,000 feet above water. It appears like a gigantic obelisk, or a pyramid rising from the ocean and extending into the clouds. I'm a woman. Grey of hair. Solitary. Reclusive, even. But generous towards those with whom she shares a bond. And here, the origin of all things descends not from a single creator, but from a state of chaos. From darkness. *Fan-a-ooou Po*. It means, born of night. And I feel I am surrounded by invisible intelligences.

Fugue state

The shadow of the bread fruit leaf is cast, trembling, shaken by the power of the arm of Ta'aroa. It passes over the goddess Hine, and from that shadow Oro, the god of war, comes into being.

Here's something cool, smooth. Metal? Perhaps stone.
I want to say metallic, but the sensation is softer, paper-like.
It's a harbour somewhere. And I feel that you are in awe of this place.
Entranced.
Bewitched, even. Or something like that, I want to say.
It's not your home. Perhaps nowhere are you at home.
I'm sensing that something is radically altered. That this is desired, a desired affect.
And I feel I want to be with others, maybe so I can disappear. Do you understand? So I want to stay. I am planning to return, through the grafted shrubbery, silver, skin and financial complications to be, to just be. On my own terms, on my own, to be with them, be... them.

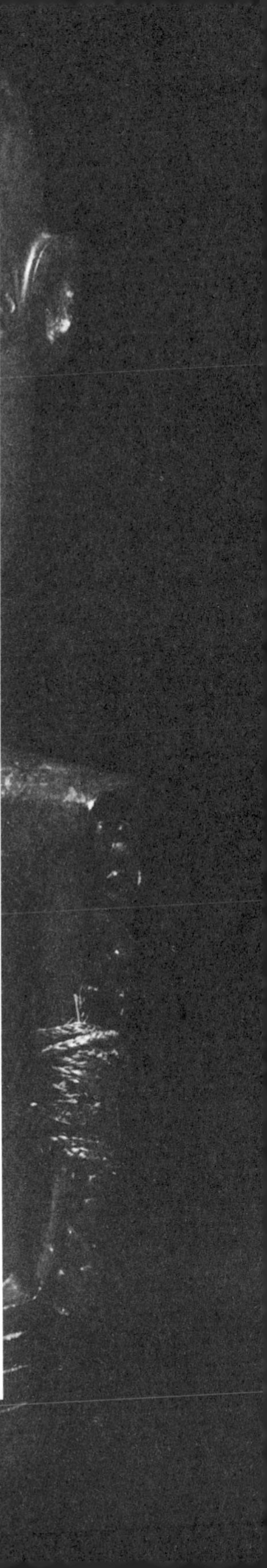

Smoke?

I found an account of the bungalow recently. It said all that remained of the house were the large stone pillars, the supporting structures. But this is from the 1950s, I think. I couldn't see it in Google Maps.

The writer commented, in a way that betrays some kind of palpable arousal brought about by the irony of it all, on the ruin's resemblance to a place of sacrifice. But seriously, you built it on a desolate ancient temple, a sacred *marae*, yes? Greta Garbo tried to rent it out after the crash, but whoever came to stay at the house moved immediately out again. Depressing and haunted, they say. Rumours about the tenants were rife. I was back in Berlin at the time, but I heard them: the single woman who committed suicide after three days; the newlyweds who departed after one week, on separate boats. And poor Douglas Fairbanks. Actually, he really did get a fright. But then, it burnt down. Problem solved, I suppose. That was the last of the incidents. First, it was the cook's death. Then the camera lost on the reef, the Mota Tapu night-filming accident, Colorart bailing out on the cash for *Tabu*, the headache with Bob Flaherty, the car...

And I am feeling, freaky chance?
          Wrath of the gods?
And I want to say,
          destiny?

With the accumulation of each event, my understanding of the subsequent events as occurring by chance though, begins to feel less probable and more meaningful. And, by the time you get to the end of the constellatory chain, there's this impression of an existing foreknowledge that

A female figure from Tahiti, pr
ably associated with househ
worship.

of the Hawaiian chain to the other. In a famous contest with six other professionals, in which each had to completely fill a house

he fished up lands, stole fire, snared the sun, controlled the winds and arranged the stars. Not that his contemporaries were all that

cannot be attributed to chance. A weird synchronicity of things or motifs. A phenomena of a-causal, meaningful coincidences: where a psychic, affective state corresponds with a concrete future event, and this event, by its very nature of being not yet existent, is verifiable only afterwards. So it gains momentum? Gravity.

So what you are feeling is a sense of synchronicity – a parallelism of time and meaning between psychic and psychophysical events.

cook dead
camera lost
Mota Tapu
no cash
headache Bob
the car...

We understand cause and effect as the basis of science and rationalism, yes? So can we – we can therefore think of synchronistic events because they are a-causal, as existing outside the bounds of the geometric reality of time and space.

So synchronicity is irrational?

A-causal.
Unverifiable.

And yet, a house was built. A camera was lost. A film was filmed. Hands were burnt while filming that film. That film about a tabu.

It is a complex fragrance. Palm, plastic, fruity, oil? Accentuated by wet heat. There is also a table, a large circular table constructed from a dense pinky-yellow hardwood, by hands. It's an impressive object.

A centrepiece, maybe, around which activity orbits. The surface of the polished tabletop is collecting and casting into my eyes lovely violent spectra from all angles.

as yet unknown. Maui set out to rectify this state of affairs with considerable enthusiasm and sometimes near-disastrous repercussions. He helped to raise the skies;

laughed. The Marquesan and the Tuomotuan narratives were distinctly erotic in style. In Tonga there was much elaboration of monster slaying incidents. In the Society

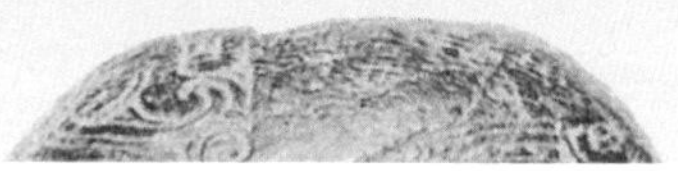

Maori tiki or ancestor figure. The Maoris sometimes commemorated their ancestors by figure carving or by bas-relief carving on panels. ly the face was tatooed; the borate marking on the body of figure represents the joints. tish Museum.

Where was I?
Here. OK, yes. The scent is contained, not actualised into humid form. An ash cloud, I want to say.
But it's more a smog or a thick film of opaque red and silver and orange.
And it's also producing a voice, a tone rather, uttered in the spirit of amusement. The tabued need not necessarily believe in the tabu in order for it to take effect.
It does seem causal.
But not exactly in a 'you don't pay your bills, your mobile gets disconnected' kind of way though, is it?
Is it?

I am approaching the edge of a promontory. From the road. And the shape of the ocean is singular, imposing.
I want to say, death does not lie.
And neither did the clairvoyant, seemingly.

> *You will arrive in Germany on the 4 April 1931, but not in the way you expect.*

So, now I'm thinking, I'd better cheat fate and go by boat instead. But then it was not on the way back home to see Mother, but driving up to Monterey, before the premiere of *Tabu* in New York, to talk to whoever that was about the adaptation – that was when it happened.
He can't drive. Too ugly. Garcia, you drive.
Garcia, Garcia, Garcia. He's really beautiful. Wow. Almost as magnificent as Matahi. But a terrible driver. Audacious and insolent. Needless to say, the Rolls Royce didn't fare well either. But despite what Kenneth Anger claimed, I was not going down on Garcia at that time.
Eight plane crashes in World War One. Not a scratch.
Cruising in the back of the Rolls with a ten-year Paramount

erleaf, left: a double-figured tiki a Maori house. The Maoris ›lied the word tiki, meaning *man*, these carved human figures ich were used as gable orna- nts. Hooper Collection.

erleaf, centre: a Rarotongan ff god. These averaged about teen feet in length though some e longer. They consisted of an ɔer carved portion with a profile d surmounting a series of figures ernately profile and full-face; a ddle section wrapped round with a cloth until it was two or ee yards in circumference; and erminal phallus. The missionary n Williams reports seeing many n to pieces before his eyes, some were saved and sent to gland. Usually only the upper tion has survived. Many of se images are thought to be of ɔ, son of Tangaroa, but some estigators believe they represent ngaroa himself.

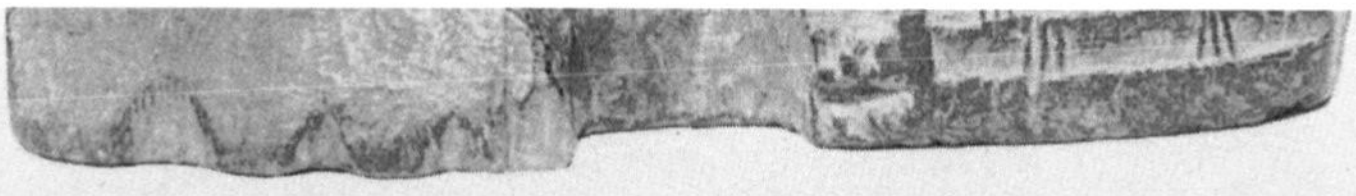

Overleaf, right: one of the rare short hula drums from Hawaii, supported by a carved frieze of figures. Hooper Collection.

contract, Garcia glancing back at me, that glorious West Coast sunset at El Capitan Canyon. The silver-plated spirit of ecstasy channels into dirt and sand here, wings extended and head tilted in reminiscence of the take-off.

I never know whether to believe or not. Belief implies a doubt anyway, as opposed to sensing or knowing. Feeling is knowing. And if you want to feel it,

all you have to do is be it.

But it was committed to nitrocellulose in any case. I can assure you though, that in fact the whole subject is highly obscure. It's something that is altogether unapproachable. Think of it as a spectrum of unapproachability. At one end you have the sacred, the divine and the consecrated and, at the other, we have the uncanny, the dangerous and the profane. It's a quality that can be attributed to practically anything – to the dead, to the spirits, to that thing, to this person, to a Lamborghini. It is the natural and direct result of *mana*, the Polynesian mystical force, being or state. All tabu objects must contain *mana*; and most *mana* objects are tabu. A tabu can be acquired indirectly or it can be imposed.

Objectively speaking, they are prohibitions. And the violation of one, unwitting or otherwise, makes the offender (her or himself) tabu. It can be passed on, not only via physical contact or imposition, but via an indexical nature too. Through shadows, for example. So in this sense, the transference of a tabu can happen as the shadow of one person,

a tabued person,

falls onto to the body or the shadow of the next.

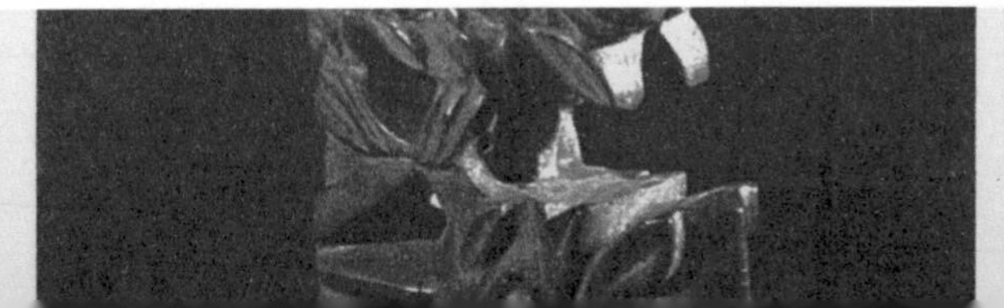

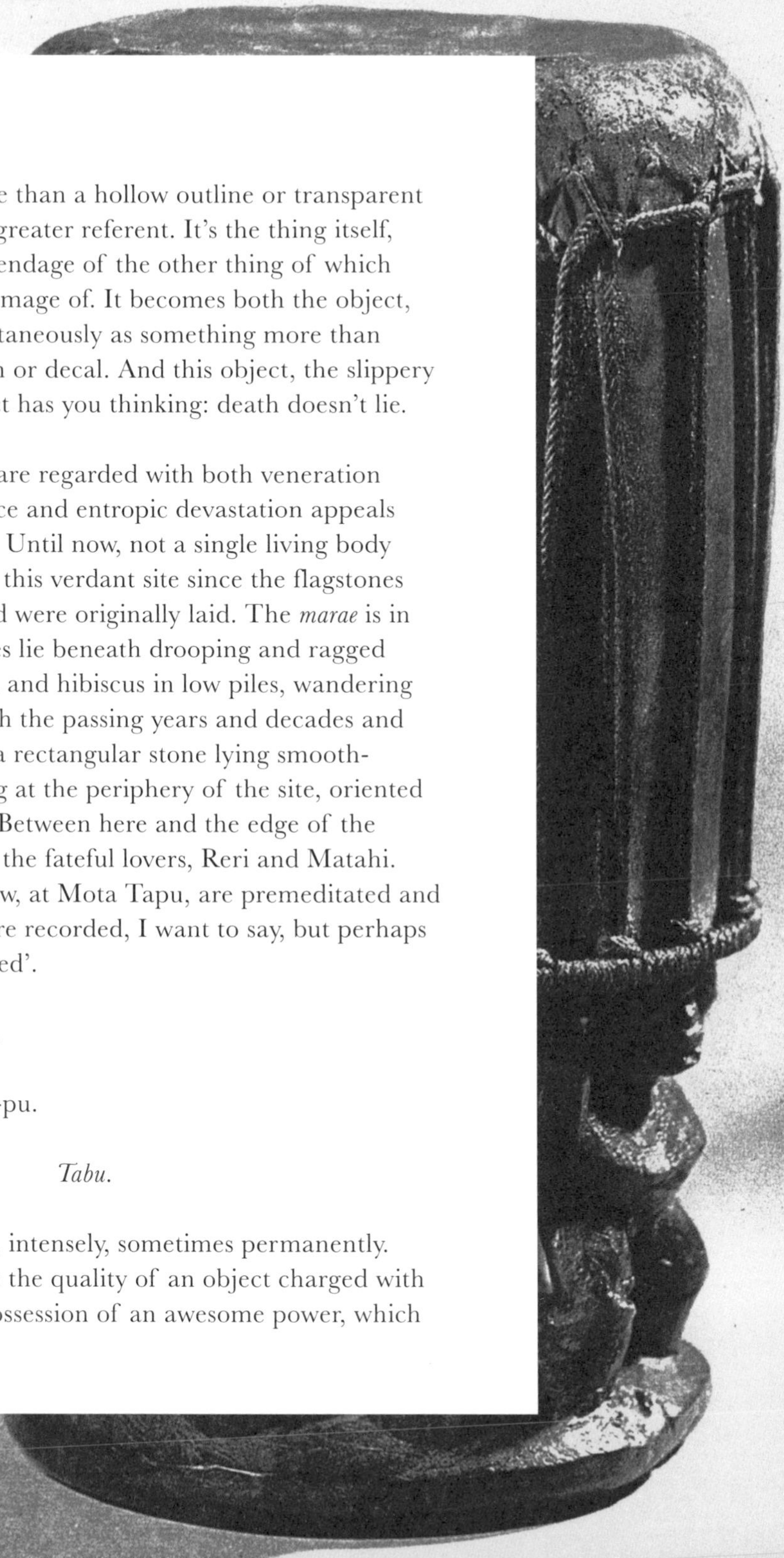

In an instant.
This shadow is more than a hollow outline or transparent indication of some greater referent. It's the thing itself, but it is also an appendage of the other thing of which it is the shadow, or image of. It becomes both the object, and an object simultaneously as something more than mere approximation or decal. And this object, the slippery quality of this object has you thinking: death doesn't lie.

In Tahiti, the dead are regarded with both veneration and horror. Romance and entropic devastation appeals to your sensibilities. Until now, not a single living body has ventured across this verdant site since the flagstones of the burial ground were originally laid. The *marae* is in ruin. Its fallen stones lie beneath drooping and ragged clusters of gardenia and hibiscus in low piles, wandering slowly outwards with the passing years and decades and centuries. There is a rectangular stone lying smooth-surfaced and glaring at the periphery of the site, oriented towards the ocean. Between here and the edge of the water, I'm perusing the fateful lovers, Reri and Matahi. Things here and now, at Mota Tapu, are premeditated and accumulative; they're recorded, I want to say, but perhaps it's more 'precipitated'.

Taaa-puuu.

Ta-pu.

Tabu.

Marked thoroughly, intensely, sometimes permanently. Things tabued have the quality of an object charged with electricity and in possession of an awesome power, which

enchanted axe, Great Helve of Hibiscus Wood, but he had chosen a tapu tree in the sacred valley and it was lifted up again by

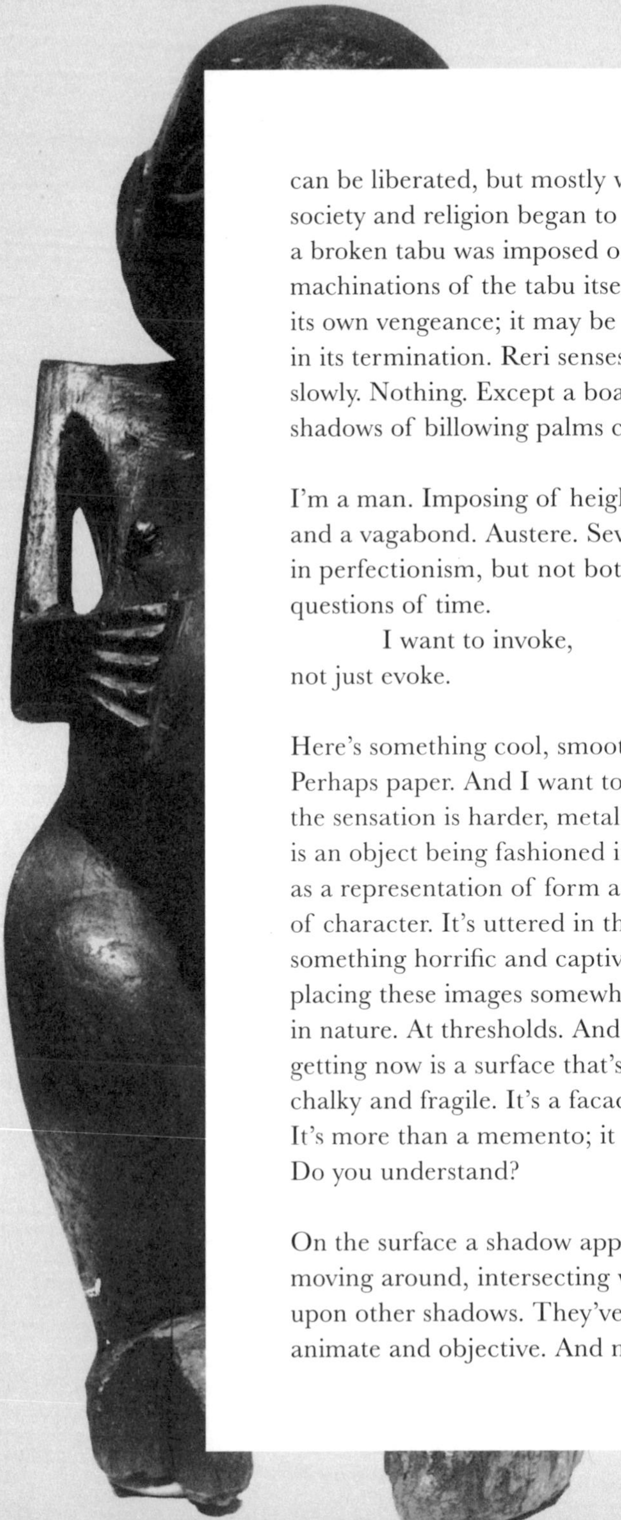

can be liberated, but mostly with destructive effect. Before society and religion began to intervene, the punishment for a broken tabu was imposed only by the internal, autonomous machinations of the tabu itself. In other words, the tabu seeks its own vengeance; it may be gradual in its progress but fatal in its termination. Reri senses something, and you turn around slowly. Nothing. Except a boat cutting through water and the shadows of billowing palms cast onto the sand.

I'm a man. Imposing of height. A fugitive and a vagabond. Austere. Severe. Tireless in perfectionism, but not bothered with questions of time.

I want to invoke,
not just evoke.

Here's something cool, smooth. Wood? Perhaps paper. And I want to say paper, but the sensation is harder, metallic. And there is an object being fashioned into a likeness, as a representation of form and emblem of character. It's uttered in the tone of something horrific and captivating. I'm placing these images somewhere transitional in nature. At thresholds. And what I'm getting now is a surface that's white, hard, chalky and fragile. It's a facade, an index. It's more than a memento; it is its own thing. Do you understand?

On the surface a shadow appears. It's moving around, intersecting with and acting upon other shadows. They've become animate and objective. And now they jump

the evident homogeneity of mythological themes, in spite of the separation of island groups from each other in both time and distance. But when the myths of a particular group are considered separately a different pattern emerges. Culture heroes show dif-

ual favours. The premium placed on female attractiveness also influenced child-feeding methods. Babies were not breastfed; pre-

from one conduit to another. And they find and occupy their own image.

Now you cast your own shadow and slip out of shot. Destiny is rendered? Paranormal tragedy takes place.

In the film…or?
I want to say.

t: a carved wooden figure from iiti. These figures were not re- sentations of the gods; they e used by sorcerers who had the ver to summon the spirit to enter image.

Vebber, artist of Captain Cook's d voyage, recorded the bring- of gifts to the Captain from the ng of Owyhee. The foremost ible canoe, with its crab-claw ped sail made of plaited pan- as leaf strips, carried the nobles their feather cloaks and helmets. other carried three draped fig- s on the platform between the hulls. British Museum.

Charlotte Prodger

Say what you see

Three Voices – Gregg Bordowitz

'Three Voices', composed by Morton Feldman, for solo voice and two prerecorded solo voices, performed at the Museum of Modern Art, New York, 4 March 2013 as part of the exhibition Inventing Abstraction, 1910–1925.

Fade up from black. A video monitor on a shelf. On the shelf in black marker pen: FACTORY COMMUNICATIONS 26/3/85. On the monitor screen is a video of the digital counter and keys of a sampler. The digital counter is counting upward: 11.06.52
53
54
55

To the left of the video monitor in orange Helvetica is the name of the track. To the right of the video monitor in orange Helvetica: Fac 321.

Dry ice obscures the monitor but the orange titles remain. The dry ice cross-dissolves to grey matte. The grey matte cross-dissolves to a woman's head and shoulders. She is out of focus. She steps forward into focus. The orange titles disappear.

The woman has short dark hair. She wears a pink mohair jumper with an asymmetrical neckline, and large black circular earrings. She wears red lipstick, green eyeshadow, mascara. She is looking off camera, down and slightly to the right. She straightens her back.

Cut to a head and shoulders shot of a man in a denim shirt with a white T-shirt beneath. A vocal microphone is pointing at his mouth. There's a black leather guitar strap across his left shoulder. His eyes move around, conspicuously avoiding the camera. His hair is streaked blonde on top. On the sides, where it's shorter, it is dark brown. He licks his lips, twitches his head, and looks down. Cut to the head and shoulders of a man with short brown hair. He wears a black jumper with three black buttons along the left shoulder. He bobs slightly in time to the beat. His eyes avoid the camera. He keeps looking to his left, and then down. His mouth opens slightly, then closes.

Cut to the head and shoulders of a bearded man. His facial hair is red. His hair is light brown, mid-length and wavy. The top of his head is obscured by the top of the frame. He wears a black leather jacket and black T-shirt. A white plectrum protrudes from the right corner of his mouth. Its logo is partially obscured by his lip. He is looking down, moving in a staccato rhythm.

Cut to a side-on shot of both his hands playing a maroon bass guitar. Because of the depth of field, the neck of the guitar and his left hand are out of focus. The right cuff of his leather jacket is scuffed. He wears gold rings on his middle and fourth fingers. The movement of the fingers of his left hand is shadowed on his left thigh.

Cut to a shot which is empty apart from a blurred shape to the right of the frame. The woman enters the frame from the left. She is looking up. She reaches up, out of the frame, with her right arm.

Cut to a head and shoulders shot of the woman from behind reaching up with her right arm to a bank of three identical synthesizers in flight cases with open fronts. On the top synthesizer is a row of black dials. She turns the dial on the farthest right. Cut to an extreme close-up of her face. She is looking up.

Cut to the man in the denim shirt. It is the same framing as before. He is looking down and to his left. Now he looks up at the microphone. He looks down again. Now he is moving in rhythm. He holds the microphone. His movements become more pronounced. He looks to the right. His mouth is open.

Cut back to the extreme close up of the woman's face looking up. She exits the frame.

Cut. She enters the frame of another shot. She's looking down.

Cut to her hands side-on at a synthesizer keyboard. Because of the depth of field her left hand is out of focus. Only her right hand presses the keys. Her left hand holds the machine's black casing.

Cut again to the man's hands playing the maroon bass.

Cut to the man in the denim shirt. He is bobbing.

His fingers are curled round the microphone. He holds a white plectrum between index finger and thumb. He looks down, then to his left, then up. He closes his eyes. He starts to sing. The left shoulder with the leather strap raises up and down with the start of each new line. His eyes remain closed throughout the verse. He removes his hand from the microphone.

Cut to an extreme close-up of a hand on a synthesizer keyboard. E. C. E. G. C.

Cut to the head and shoulders of the man with the black buttons on his shoulder.

Cut to the man in the denim shirt, singing. He is swaying then jutting. His facial expressions are more emphatic now.

Cut to the man in the leather jacket. He moves into the shot from the right and immediately turns ninety degrees while taking a plectrum out of his mouth. In his right hand he holds two drumsticks. They jut back across his right shoulder. The camera moves down the side of his body to a drum machine at waist height. It sits at a forty-five degree angle. It's a red surface with six black hexagonal panels. Five in a circle, one in the centre. He hits the hexagonal panels with the drumsticks.

Cut to the hand on the synthesizer keyboard. Cut to the man with the black shoulder buttons. He is moving faster than before.

Cut to the man in the denim shirt. He holds a red cowbell in his left hand, hitting it with a drumstick in his right hand. The microphone is jutting into the left of the frame.

Cut to the woman. She is looking down. She looks up, then looks down again. The studio is reflected in the disc of her earring.

Cut to the man in the leather jacket. The camera is below the drum machine. The drum machine is out of focus because of the depth of field. Protruding above it is the man's face from the nose upward. The tips of the drumsticks are moving up and down rapidly. He stops, turns to his left and exits the frame.

Cut to a wide shot of the studio. The man in the leather jacket is wearing jogging pants. In the foreground is a rectangular area of black rubber flooring with loose cables laid across it. The rest of the studio floor beyond it is mauve carpet. In the centre of the carpet is a rectangle of light, from the four rectangular lights in the ceiling above. The four people are facing the same direction. The man with the denim shirt is playing a guitar adjacent to the window of the mixing booth. He moves his right leg in time. The woman is playing a synthesizer behind him. She moves her right foot in time. The man in the leather jacket and jogging pants is playing a bass guitar. He moves to and fro. Behind him is the man with the buttoned jumper playing a synthesizer. He touches his ear while jutting his head back and forth. He is partially obscured by a bank of equipment in shadow.

Cut to close-up of the maroon bass guitar being played rapidly with the white plectrum. The bass guitar moves up and down. His hand is reflected in the maroon surface.

Cut to the man in the denim shirt in front of the window of the mixing booth. He places a drumstick down next to the cowbell. His arm with its rolled-up sleeve is reflected in the glass. Watching from behind the glass is a long-haired stout man in a black jacket. His face is partially obscured by the microphone in front of the glass. To the right of him, the woman is reflected, but more faintly.

Partially obscured by the man in the denim shirt, there is a white A3 poster on the wall displaying two words in black. The blocky font has been designed to appear three-dimensional, as if being viewed from below.

The man picks up a plectrum from beside the cowbell and begins to play a black guitar.

Cut to the man in the leather jacket rapidly playing the maroon bass. The grey fabric of his jogging pants moves forward and back. A curl of hair above his collar moves in syncopated rhythm. Behind him is a large mixing desk, and behind that an open door with light shining through it. A man leans against the doorframe, watching with his arms folded. His form is unclear because of the depth of field and over-exposure. He nods his head in time.

Cut to the man in the denim shirt playing the black guitar hung high on his waist. His right hand makes wide downward arcs across the guitar, punctuated by a staccato strumming action. He moves left and right in the frame.

Cut to the man in the leather jacket.

Cut to the man in the denim shirt moving faster.

Cut to a right hand on a keyboard.

Cut to the man in the leather jacket playing the maroon bass high on the neck. He looks to his right.

Cut to the man in the denim shirt. He moves his left hand quickly up the neck of the guitar, then stops playing. He looks to his left.

Cut to the man in the leather jacket. Leaning back, he moves his left hand incrementally down the neck of the maroon bass, then stops playing.

Cut to an extreme close-up of a hand on a keyboard. The index finger presses the key on the farthest right. It holds it, then drops down and moves out of the frame.

Cut to the face of the man in the black-buttoned jumper. He looks to his right.

Cut to the face of the man in the denim shirt. He looks to his left.

Cut to the face of the man in the leather jacket. He looks ahead at the camera.

Cut to the face of the woman. She walks out of shot, leaving behind an out of focus surface of various overlapping shapes.

In the top of the frame, in orange Helvetica, fade in the words Henri Alekan. To their right appear the words Alan Butler. Below Henri Alekan appear the words Louis Cochet. To their right, Jonathan Demme. A further 26 names appear in the same way, creating two columns. At the bottom of the left column, Fac 321 fades in. All the names fade out. Fac 321 remains. The surface of overlapping shapes fades to black. Fac 321 fades out. Black leader remains for 3 seconds.

On the morning of 4 July 2013, I walked down the baking streets of Manhattan's Lower East Side with Dena in search of air conditioning and a place to talk over what we might each contribute to the next issue of *The Happy Hypocrite* which was, at that point, a blank slate. The building heat was unbearably radiant, and it was hard to think. Dena told me Manhattan's increasing draw on the national grid had affected the year-round temperature of the island to the point that its warmed soil could produce and sustain, for the first time in recorded history, fig trees.

A few weeks previous to our meeting, there had been a remarkable series of events, some local, some farther flung. A spate of brutal anti-gay assaults in the city had left a number of people hospitalised, presumed by some to be victims of an unexpected backlash against the country's increasingly open legal stance on gay marriage and the visibility of LGB people in the military*. A Democratic Senator for Texas, Wendy Davis, had worn sneakers and a back brace so she could more comfortably stand, uninterrupted and unaided for eleven hours on Capitol Hill, Washington DC, to deliver a filibuster to block an anti-abortion bill. Back in my newly relocated home of the United Kingdom, the 'legacy' talk of the London Olympic Games was switching over from a discussion of health and athleticism, to one of corporate ownership and privatisation.

Regardless of my personal views on the aforementioned sequence of events, they each felt in some way contingent. Moreover, they appeared to me particularly emphatic at a time when discussions of dematerialised labour, invisible networks, and deregulated economies were peaking in the trade presses of contemporary art.

The body is our most essential material, our primary limit. It has always been subjected to change, invasion, adaptation, and enhancement. But information surrounding such intrusions seemed, in July 2013, more pronounced than ever before. Regulation of the body – whether self-imposed or via external legislation – was increasing apace. Our physiology too was changing by soft increments, though swiftly, to adapt to external technologies, and presumably continues to do so. (Among users of smart phones, for example, the musculature that supports our thumbs has developed to such a size that we substitute previous activities of our forefinger with that of our thumb – when we push a button for the pedestrian crossing, when we ring a doorbell.)

Attentive to the conditions of bodily regulation, I did not seek to find writers that dealt explicitly with such events, but rather build a temporary assembly of individuals who are acutely and intelligently aware that what we choose to do with our bodies, how we express it alone or with others, can provide valuable cultural openings and resistances to the regulation of which I speak.

* *Transgender people are barred from entering the US Military.*

— Isla Leaver-Yap, Glasgow, 24 May 2014

Isla tells me this is a user manual. Last Thursday.

Kathy Acker responds to Mark McGill's twenty-ninth question 'Is your memory: a) Exceptional b) Good c) Normal d) Bad c) Senile' with the answer 'Let's compare a pencil to a vagina'. *BOMB* 1983.

Soft-tissue metaphor appealing as the inside meaning of it, the mystery of body through space, function of breath corroding the very buildings built to shelter us. Those words I have just written, I am speaking them aloud, to test where the breath is headed, I believe it goes upward.

I report with joy that Isla Leaver-Yap is *The Happy Hypocrite's* second guest-editor. For this, the seventh issue of the journal – tantalisingly themed Heat Island – Isla is inviting a temporary community of fourteen contributors, unidirectional in method, to find ways to try to come together: discussing, hallucinating, imagining, refilling, summoning bodies. This is a necessary task, one of serious speculation certainly, for our corporeal selves exist as cycles we have but little knowledge of. Just like Proteus in *Demon Seed* we may ask 'When are you going to let me out this box?' but the material truth is that we will be interred in this box long before we will ever be able to be let out of it.

Thus we must act while we can.

— Maria Fusco, Edinburgh, May 2014

THE LIST

— Book Works Supporter's Scheme

Book Works is a publicly funded organisation dedicated to commissioning contemporary artist's books, projects and exhibitions. Founded in 1984, and celebrating their 30th anniversary this year, Book Works has worked with a diverse range of artists – often as emerging artists, publishing for the first time, many of whom have gone on to great success: Tacita Dean, Jeremy Deller, Mark Dion, Douglas Gordon, Liam Gillick, Susan Hiller, Joseph Kosuth, Slavs and Tatars, Katrina Palmer, Sarah Pierce, Adrian Piper, Elizabeth Price, Dora García and Laure Prouvost. We also have a history of commissioned projects with guest editors and curators including: Mark Beasley, Isla Leaver-Yap, Lisa Le Feuvre, Nav Haq, Matthew Higgs, Lynne Tillman, Federica Bueti, Stewart Home, Stefan Kalmár, Lisa Panting, Francesco Pedraglio, Nina Power and Sara Wajid.

The List is a vital part of our organisation's success. Our friends and supporters are often drawn from artists, designers and curators that we've worked with, as well as friends, business colleagues, art collectors and our wider readership and audience. It forms a community and network that gives value and support, both financially and in terms of critique, review, discussion, and further opportunities. We have an ongoing need to raise a substantial contribution towards our annual programme from like-minded individuals and organisations prepared to support Book Works' commitment to developing new art projects and working with artists at all stages of there careers.

Benefits supporters include: invitations to launches and events, mailing of our annual catalogue and a discount on Book Works publications.

The List

A Friend ☐ Annual Rate £35 ☐ Concessionary student rate £20

A Supporter ☐ Annual Rate £100 ☐ A Gallery or Business Supporter Annual Rate £500

Friends and Supporters of Book Works will be acknowledged on our website and annual catalogue, receive a catalogue, invitations to all launches and a 10% discount on all Book Works' publications, prints and special editions.

A Patron ☐ Annual Rate £1,000

Patrons of Book Works contribute £1,000 and above each year. In addition to our other benefits, Patrons will be invited to meet commissioned artists, attend special events associated with our programme and to our annual Book Works event.

A Project Patron ☐ £5,000 and above

Project Patrons help to fund a specific publication, curatorial residency, or exhibition and have the opportunity for close association with the development of the project. They receive all Patrons' benefits plus acknowledgement on all materials associated with the project.

To Join *The List*, please visit: www.bookworks.org.uk/support
or send your payment to Book Works, 19 Holywell Row, London EC2A 4JB

For more information please contact Gavin Everall: 020 7247 2203/gavin@bookworks.org.uk

For payment by credit card we need the following information:

Card Type

☐ M/C ☐ Visa ☐ Switch ☐ Visa Debit

Card Number ______________________

Name on Card ______________________

Billing Address (including full postcode)

____

____

____

____

Telephone No. ______________________

Email ______________________

Expiry Date ______________________

Start Date ______________________

Issue Number (Switch only) ______________

Security Code (3 digits) ______________

Alternatively, please make cheques (£ sterling only) payable to 'Book Works (UK) Ltd' and post to the above address. Or PAYPAL, direct funds to admin@bookworks.org.uk

Elaine Cameron-Weir
is an artist currently living in New York. She received a BFA from the Alberta College of Art and Design, Alberta, Canada, and an MFA from New York University, New York. Among other places, she has exhibited in Philadelphia, New York, Cologne and Paris.

Maria Fusco
is a Belfast-born writer, editor and critic. She is author of *With A Bao A Qu Reading When Attitudes Become Form* (New Documents, 2013), *The Mechanical Copula* (Sternberg Press, 2010) and forthcoming *Legend of the Necessary Dreamer* (Copy Press, 2014). She is a Hawthornden Fellow, has been invited to be writer-in-residence at Kadist Art Foundation, Paris; Lisbon Architecture Triennale; Whitechapel Gallery, London, and is a Reader at Edinburgh College of Art, University of Edinburgh, previously acting as Director of Art Writing at Goldsmiths, University of London. *mariafusco.net*

Allison Gibbs
is an Australian-born artist working with film, video, writing and extra-sensory activity. She is currently based in Glasgow.

Will Holder
Typographer Will Holder produces publications with artists and musicians, and is preoccupied with conversation as model and tool for a mutual and improvised set of publishing conditions – whereby the usual roles of commissioner, author, subject, editor, printer and typographer are improvised and shared, as opposed to assigned and pre-determined. Particular attention is placed on an oral production of value and meaning around cultural objects, and how live, extra-informational qualities might be analysed, documented and scored. Based in London, Holder is editor of *F.R.DAVID*, a journal concerned with reading and writing in the arts (published by de Appel, Amsterdam, since 2007). Together with Alex Waterman, he is editing and typesetting *Yes, But Is It Edible?*, a biography of American composer Robert Ashley, for four or more voices (New Documents, forthcoming, 2014).

Isla Leaver-Yap
works with artists to produce publications, projects, and events. She has recently worked with The Block, Andrea Büttner, Ellen Cantor, Lygia Clark, Moyra Davey, Pat Hearn, Emma Hedditch, Derek Jarman, Angie Keefer, Sam Korman, Lucy McKenzie, James Richards, Hannah Rickards, Ben Schumacher, Lucy Skaer, Rita Sobral Campos, Cara Tolmie, and Sue Tompkins. She is based in Glasgow where she is LUX Scotland Project Director, and Minneapolis where she is the Walker Art Center's Bentson Film Scholar.

Duncan Marquiss
is an artist and musician based in Glasgow who makes drawings and films. He is currently interested in analogies between biological processes and creative work. Recent exhibitions include *Spandrels*, The Pipe Factory, Glasgow, 2014; *Flatness: Cinema After The Internet*, Kurzfilmtage, Oberhausen, 2013; and *Secret Societies*, Schirn Kunsthalle, Frankfurt, 2011.

Park McArthur
lives in New York. Her work has been exhibited at The Kitchen, New York; Essex Street, New York; Catherine Bastide, Brussels; Lars Friedrich, Berlin. Her writing has been included in the *International Journal of Feminist Approaches to Bioethics* and the *Movement Research Performance Journal*. 'Other forms of conviviality: the best and least of which is our daily care, the most of which is our collaborative work', an essay co-written with Constantina Zavitsanos, was included in a special issue of *Women & Performance: A journal of feminist theory*, 'We are Born in Flames', edited by Dean Spade and Craig Willse.

Anna McLauchlan
studied Fine Art at Duncan of Jordanstone College of Art and Design, served on the committee of Glasgow's Transmission Gallery and has subsequently trained in environmental studies and hatha yoga. Anna is a Teaching Associate in Geography at the University of Strathclyde, a hatha yoga teacher, and part of the artist-run group The Strickland Distribution.

Giuseppe Mistretta
is unsure of where he's heading but is enjoying the journey. Recent projects include: *Dance like nobody's watching* or *Dance like you're not dancing*; Rhubaba Gallery and Studios, Edinburgh; *Gnommero-Visibility*, edited by Sarah Tripp and Richard Taylor; *Lights Out Listening Group*, The Old Hairdressers, Glasgow; *Muscle Memory*, The Walled Garden, Glasgow (with Claire Shallcross); *unsmoothmaking*, Transmission Gallery, Glasgow, and Lothringer13_Laden, Munich (with Sarah Forrest and Psykick Dancehall); Stories, The Task, Melbourne; *The Braille Room*, Intermedia Gallery, Glasgow.

Paul Nash (1889–1946)
was a writer, artist and designer. He was the first individual to be given the title of British War Artist, producing artwork in response to both the First and Second World Wars. He was a member of the Omega Workshop and Unit One. A prolific writer, he also authored *Dorset: A Shell Guide*, edited by John Betjeman, 1936.

Charlotte Prodger
is based in Glasgow. Solo exhibitions include Studio Voltaire, London; Intermedia, Kendall Koppe, and Glasgow International, all Glasgow. Group exhibitions and performances include Artists Space, New York; Tramway, Glasgow; Pieter Performance Space, Los Angeles; Hotel, London; Essex Street, New York; Lux Biennial of Moving Images, ICA, London; Temporary Gallery, Cologne; Poor Farm, Wisconsin; Pillar Corrias, London. Prodger's writing has been published in *2HB* and *F.R.DAVID*. Residencies include Cove Park, Wysing Arts Centre, and Hospitalfield. Forthcoming solo exhibitions include *Markets*, a presentation by The Block at Chelsea Space, London, 2014; Inverleith House, 2015, touring to Spike Island, Bristol; and Temple Bar, Dublin. In 2013, she was shortlisted for the Jarman Award.

Francis Sanzaro (Ph.D.)
believes that all practice, whether it is artistic, philosophical or athletic, must begin and end with a profound sense of joy. Based out of Baltimore, Maryland, Francis' work stems from a direct engagement with the arts, theory, and an attempt to articulate the body's intelligence in ways as of yet unspoken. He writes poetry and fiction during his lunch breaks. His articles and fiction have appeared in *Continental Philosophy Review, Greyrock Review, Sierra Nevada Review, Rock and Ice, The Baltimore Post Examiner, Journal for Cultural and Religious Theory, Words and Numbers, 8a.nu*, and *DAASN*, among others. His most recent publications include a book on athletic theory and the body, titled *The Boulder: A Philosophy for Bouldering* (Stone Country Press, 2013).

Mary Simpson
was born in Anchorage, Alaska and currently lives in New York. She received an MFA from Columbia University and attended the Whitney Independent Study Program. Her work has shown at On Stellar Rays, Bortolami Gallery, Rachel Uffner Gallery, all New York; Almine Rech, Brussels; Hilary Crisp, London; Seattle Art Museum; Boise Art Museum. Films screenings, projects and lectures include the Artists Institute, The Kitchen, both New York; Henry Art Gallery, Seattle; CAM2, Madrid. She teaches at Cooper Union and Columbia University.

Stow College, Glasgow
was established in 1934 as a 'trades school' by the now defunct Corporation of Glasgow Education Department. Named after David Stow (1793–1864), a Victorian pioneer of learning and teacher training, Stow College was Glasgow's first purpose-built college and initially offered evening classes. This issue of the *Happy Hypocrite* reproduces selected specimens

of commercial printing by the students of Stow College's School of Printing. The original specimen portfolio was found and bought in a second hand bookshop in 2012 because it was initially perceived to be a book about the golden age of Greek sculpture.

Dena Yago
is an artist and writer based in New York City. Her recent exhibitions include *Heat Island*, Gasconade, Milan (2014), and she has forthcoming exhibitions at Eli Ping, New York (2014), and a collaborative work with artist Laurie Spiegel at Cubitt Gallery, London (2014). Yago's book of poetry, *Ambergris*, will be published through Bodega Press later this year. Along with four other artists and writers, she is a producer of *K-HOLE*, an annually released trend forecasting report.

SEEKING
ACCELERATED
MATERIALS.
LUBRICATE
HERE.

Issue 1 'Linguistic Hardcore'
Spring / Summer 2008

Issue 2 'Hunting and Gathering'
Autumn / Winter 2008

Issue 3 'Volatile Dispersal'
Spring / Summer 2009

Issue 4 'A Rather Large Weapon'
Autumn / Winter 2009

Issue 5 'What am I?'
Spring / Summer 2010

Issue 6 'Freedom'
Guest edited by Lynne Tillman
Autumn 2013

Available to order from www.bookworks.org.uk

ALBE DE COKER.

Printed by Albe de Coker
Industrieterrein Polderstad, Boombekelaan 12
BE-2660 Antwerpen (Hoboken)
Enquiries to Hugh Jolly/hugh.jolly@icloud.com
www.albedecoker.com